THE PAN BOOK OF
PARTY GAMES

THE PAN BOOK OF
PARTY GAMES

JOSEPH EDMUNDSON

**A NEW BOOK EXPRESSLY WRITTEN FOR
PAN BOOKS LTD : LONDON**

First published 1958 by
PAN BOOKS LIMITED,
8 Headfort Place, London, S.W.1

2nd Printing 1958
3rd Printing 1959
4th Printing 1960
5th Printing 1961

© 1958 by Joseph Edmundson

Line illustrations in the
text by
PATRICIA MEARES

Printed in Great Britain by Richard Clay and Company, Ltd.,
Bungay, Suffolk

CONTENTS

SECTION ONE

GIVING A PARTY

Generally speaking, the more spontaneous and carefree a party appears to a guest, the better it will be enjoyed, but to achieve spontaneity requires considerable and careful preparation beforehand—otherwise there will be awkward gaps when groups of children and adults will be left doing nothing at all and the result might well be boredom—and your reputation as a party giver will be lost.

No hard-and-fast rules can be given on the way to run a party; much will depend upon the occasion, the age of those invited, and the amount of space available. Here, however, are some general rules which can be used as guidance.

CHILDREN'S PARTIES

With children up to the age of five there is no need to work out an elaborate programme at all. With very young children of three or four all that is necessary is to provide them with your own children's toys and let them play amongst themselves for most of the time. At moments when most of them seem to be losing interest, or minor squabbles break out (as they will) gather them all together and play a simple game such as *Ring a ring o' Roses*, *Musical Bumps*, or *Oranges and Lemons*. Peace and enjoyment will quickly be restored—then allow them to play on their own again. At this young age, perhaps the most important things to them are the provision of a good tea with the inevitable jelly and ice cream, plus a balloon and a small present to take home—even if it is only a small bag of sweets or a bar of chocolate.

It is also a good idea to present small prizes to the winners of the simple games, but the prizes should be trivial ones and the giving should not be overdone. (Even at this young age the born 'pot-hunter' will be discovered.)

Try also to ensure that when prizes are given, it is not always the same child who gets them. This may need a little judicious cheating on your part in spotting winners, but in the interests of harmony and lots of peace and goodwill, it is well worth while.

Amongst the children invited, there will always be the 'little horror' who wants to bounce on furniture or fight with the others and the shy young man or maiden who shows the greatest reluctance to play anything at all.

With the first-named shocker one must exercise considerable tact and diplomacy and try to guide his high spirits (?) into the organised channels of some game or task which will stop him from breaking up your home. The shy child should be coaxed to take part in the games, but if coaxing is of little avail, let him (or her) enjoy himself in his own way. If too much pressure is put on such a child tears will almost certainly flow.

With children from about six to nine years of age quite a number of games can and should be played, and included amongst these can be simple writing ones. These should be interspersed between the more active running or chasing games, not only as a simple disciplinary measure but also to avoid your own nerves becoming completely frayed.

These quieter games are also essential for a short period after the meal—otherwise someone is bound to be sick!

Between the ages of nine and fifteen, more and more general organisation will become necessary, though many of the games will almost certainly be suggested and even organised by the children themselves; they will by this time have a fair repertoire of activities gained from previous parties and from school experience.

There will be a *slightly* lessened desire to rush madly about all the time and a greater willingness, particularly amongst the girls, to play 'brainy' games involving pencil and paper.

There will be, however, a growing tendency to self-consciousness and awkwardness amongst some of the children, due to the onset of adolescence; there will also be a growing desire for 'mixed' games in which boy partners girl. Games of this nature should therefore figure quite prominently in any programme you draw up; you must, however, use all your tact and diplomacy to prevent too much of the 'boy meets girl' atmosphere by including games which involve the mixing of partners.

TEENAGE PARTIES

In parties for young people of this often difficult age, one must accept the fact that boy has probably met girl, but at the same time the party must be planned so that boy meets other girl and girl meets other boy. In other words, there must be games which involve partners of the young people's own choice and games in which partners are changed. Music in the modern idiom (Rock 'n' Roll, at the time of writing) also plays an important part in the lives of modern teenagers, and some attempt must be made to cater for it, even if only by the introduction of some musical game in which the latest type of music is played or sung.

Care must also be taken in the selection of games, particularly games which might involve some boy or girl looking foolish. Generally, it is advisable to avoid this type of game or to reduce the number to an absolute minimum. Pencil and paper games can be played to advantage as well as the more sophisticated types of games such as *Murder* (*see* page 130), *The Horror Game* (page 152), and games derived from popular radio or television programmes such as 'Twenty Questions' or 'What's my line?'.

Treasure hunts too, providing the clues match the general intelligence of the players, can be very popular, particularly if the players work with partners of their own choice.

The great danger in a teenage party is to allow any over-emphasis of the 'boy *has* met girl' to develop. There are many young people at this age who are prepared to enjoy themselves at a party merely by sitting in a corner holding hands and looking into someone's eyes.

This must be stopped, otherwise some members of the party are liable to be embarrassed. Tact and diplomacy must be used to prevent it developing too much; perhaps the best way is publicly to ignore it but at the same time gently, jocularly, if needs be, involve the pair in some active game where it is impossible to hold the same person's hand or look into the same beautiful eyes all the time.

ADULT PARTIES

Much will depend upon the characters of the guests invited, but in general, normal adults are quite prepared to enjoy the most foolish games.

It is essential, however, to start with a few 'mixers' (*see* pages 35–40) in order to thaw out the traditional reserve of so many adults. In most parties there will be the almost inevitable 'life and soul of the party'. This person, usually a male, can be a mixed blessing. If he is allowed a completely free hand he can well ruin all your carefully thought-out schemes, and before you know where you are, it is *his* party and not yours, and sometimes (unfortunately) his party is quite a good one.

The only effective way to deal with this gentleman is to enlist his aid in running your party and give him as much to do as possible. A tactful 'Will you help me with this game, Charlie?' or 'Charles, dear, will you run *Murder* for me, you do it *so* well?' and he will almost literally eat out of your hand.

As with teenagers, the games for adults must be mixed to include the more riotous and the quieter games. Where old people are present ('Grandma always likes to come, you know') care must be taken to see that they, too, are kept amused. Some old people are quite prepared to sit, watch, and laugh at the antics of their sons and daughters, but if there is room it is often advisable to arrange a quiet game of cards for those who can no longer rush about.

One word of warning about card games. There are many people who have strong and sincere objection to playing card games of any kind, and most particularly those where there is money (however small) at stake. Their objections must always be respected—in no circumstances try to press them into doing something they have no desire to do. This same rule of course, must be applied to other games, particularly those where there is the possibility of someone either having to make a fool of themselves or being made to look a little foolish by others.

Try to inveigle, coax, and cajole your guests to participate in the most excellent games you have arranged for their hilarious amusement—but in no circumstances try to batter, bully, or bludgeon a reluctant guest into doing something against which he shows a strong objection.

If you get a real shocker who won't do anything, the ultimate remedy is always in your hands. Don't invite him again. He probably wouldn't come, anyway—but don't take the risk.

In the following pages you will find a fairly wide selection of games suitable for all ages and also for special occasions, such as wet days at the seaside when the children are often bored to tears and everyone is wishing they hadn't come, for the long car journey, and for that one fine summer day when you go for a picnic or down to the beach.

There are, of course, many more games which you may know and which are not included here, but some of those that are in this book may well be new to you—and perhaps even more important, can be adapted, or may give you an idea for another game of your own invention which will be just the thing for Willie's birthday party.

SECTION TWO

PARTIES FOR SPECIAL OCCASIONS

Most parties centre round special occasions, such as birthdays, house warmings, wedding anniversaries, or are run on certain festival days, such as St Valentine's, Twelfth Night, Guy Fawkes Night, or New Year's Eve. There are, of course, people who like giving parties just for the sheer fun of it and are even prepared to throw a party for the illogical reason that there is no excuse for having a party.

On all these festival occasions the game content of the party can be much the same, and a selection of suitable activities can be obtained from this book.

What these games cannot always give you is 'atmosphere' to suit the occasion. This 'atmosphere' can, however, often be obtained by paying special attention to such things as the nature of the invitation, by appropriate decorations, and even by the provision of special foods or dishes which are traditional for the occasion or time of year.

Below are given some notes for these occasions, which are listed chronologically and not in order of merit or importance.

NEW YEAR'S EVE

This is put first, because, though the party begins at the end of the year it goes on into the first day of the New Year.

In the north of England, Scotland (Hogmanay) and in many countries on the Continent, this festival is perhaps even more important from a party point of view than Christmas. In south-eastern England the reverse is more true.

Decorations No special ones are usually necessary, as the Christmas decorations are almost certain to be up. Cut-outs of

Father Time and a young bouncing baby (representing the New Year) can add to the occasion if desired.

Traditional Customs Certain traditional practices can be followed. (These are observed almost automatically in some parts of the country.) The ceremony of 'First Footing' demands, if luck is to be with the household during the year, that a dark man should be the first person to cross the threshold on January 1st. A careful host or hostess, bearing in mind the dire consequences of an error, will ensure that there is a dark man at the party and will see that he is put outside the door about one minute to midnight and that he will bar entry to all other people until he himself has stepped over the doorstep in the first few seconds of the New Year.

If the host is an absolute stickler for tradition, he will arm the 'First Footer' with a small lump of coal, a loaf of bread, and a Bible so that he brings with him symbolically, warmth, food, and spiritual well-being.

The host will, also traditionally, offer the obliging dark man a mince pie and a drink appropriate to the occasion and the convictions of the person involved.

A less-involved tradition, or superstition, observed in some parts of the country, is that of merely opening the back door of the house to let out the Old Year and then opening the front one to let in the New Year.

Perhaps these traditions or superstitions are foolish—who is to say?—but they certainly add atmosphere to the occasion—as does the singing of 'Auld Lang Syne'.

TWELFTH NIGHT

In olden times the eve of the Feast of Epiphany was one of the great Feast Days of the year. Now, along with St Valentine's Day, it is almost traditionally one of the great occasions for a teenage party.

Decorations On this evening it is supposed to be lucky to take down the Christmas decorations—but before this is done, a further decoration representing The Three Wise Men can be added for the occasion. These can be 'cut-outs' or made from cardboard or even pipe cleaners.

Traditions At Twelfth Night parties it is traditional to tell stories sitting round the fire; these stories, however, should not dominate the party programme, but one or two should be interspersed as quieter interludes between the more active games. As it is also traditional *and* lucky to take down decorations (and unlucky not to), this can be made the culmination of the party. Providing the weather is suitable, any unwanted decorations can be taken out into the garden and burned with ceremony. If before the party begins, some more balloons are added to the existing decorations, each member of the party could go joyfully home afterwards carrying some.

ST VALENTINE'S DAY

This is the traditional young lovers' day, and where are you likely to find love blossoming more than amongst teenagers—and therefore what better day for a party?

Decorations Hearts, cupids, and posies are quite definitely the themes on which to base your decorations. These can be cut out of pink cardboard and festooned round the walls; heart-shaped paper doyleys can also be obtained for use on the table.

Small cakes can be made heart-shaped, and even the sandwiches can be cut to a similar shape by means of the cutters available at most stores.

Traditions and Games Though the emphasis may be on young lovers, great care must be taken in the selection of games, otherwise a teenage party can become a complete flop and even most embarrassing.

There should be games, of course, where the girl and boyfriend take part as partners, but there *must* be games in which the guests take part as a whole and where the young people are compelled to participate with partners other than those with whom they came, or those they were hoping to meet. Good-humoured tolerance, a little gentle chivvying, and just a little open leg-pulling will do much to keep the flow and continuity of the party.

EASTER

This is normally the time, particularly if Easter is late, when the hostess who is giving a children's party may hope that some of the games and activities might even be held out of doors, or at least partly indoors and partly outdoors.

Decorations Easter eggs, lambs, chickens, young Teddy Bears, in fact almost any form of young life can be used as a motif for room and table decorations. In addition to the many and varied eggs which can be obtained from the shops, much can be done with ordinary eggs, hard boiled and coloured with vegetable dyes or even painted. Names of individual guests can be written or painted on these eggs, and thus a most personal note is added to the occasion.

The small prizes can also have an Easter theme; little choco-late eggs, or small bags of sugar eggs can be most attractive for both young children and adults. Jellies and blancmange made in rabbit moulds are always popular. Table decorations can be almost anything from little, yellow fluffy chicks in front of each plate to an elaborate farmyard centre thronged with the small, lifelike plastic animals which can be obtained in almost every toy shop. Incidentally, these small animals make very useful prizes as well.

An idea which will be found most attractive to small children is to make up one of the farmyard table centres suggested above. To the head or legs of each animal attach a long piece of white cotton and lead each piece of cotton either mazelike around the table to finish by each child's place (the end of the cotton should have a small tag on it bearing the name of the individual child) or draw them all together by passing them through a very small curtain ring and then fan them out so that the name tags are plainly visible.

Then, either towards the end of the meal or just before each child goes home, the children hold their name tags and pull gently to make one of the animals move. They then take home the one to which their own cotton is attached and which, of course, has moved as they pulled.

NATIONAL DAY PARTIES

People who run parties on national festivals such as St Patrick's, St David's, St Andrew's, and St George's Days need little advice on either traditions or decorations; national emblems, such as the leek, shamrock, thistle, and rose, are obvious themes.

HALLOWE'EN

This is the night traditionally associated with Witches, Black Magic, Jack o' Lanterns, Hobgoblins, and all the mysterious personages with which our superstitious ancestors

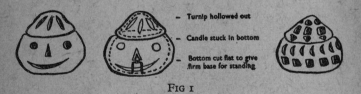

— Turnip hollowed out

— Candle stuck in bottom

— Bottom cut flat to give firm base for standing

Fig 1

peopled the dark nights, which makes it as good as, if not better than, most for the excuse to have a party.

Young and hopeful maidens, by the way, are said to be able to see the faces of their future husbands, if, on this night, they look into a mirror by candlelight. It's worth trying, you never know!

Decorations Witches in tall black hats, riding on brooms, black cats, and lanterns made from hollowed-out turnips (Fig 1) are useful for giving 'atmosphere'. The witches can be cut out of black card and pinned or taped to the curtains and walls; lanterns can be used for table decorations or can adorn the mantelpiece.

16

Traditional foods for this evening are roasted chestnuts, walnut cakes (in fact, nuts in any shape or form), and fruits, particularly apples and apple dishes.

Traditions and Games Duck Apple (*see* page 154) and *Bob Apple* (page 148) are traditional games for parties on this day; it is also an appropriate evening for (not too serious) Fortune Telling (*see* page 182). For younger children, a lantern parade around the garden often makes a fitting climax. Each child should, of course, have a lantern for this. Paper ones can be purchased quite cheaply, but if someone in the family has the time and patience to produce a turnip lantern for each child (which they are allowed to take home with them) success is assured. To make a number of turnip lanterns will take some few days, and during those days the turnips tend to shrivel and go limp. This can be prevented by soaking them in water overnight. To save all this work, it can be politely suggested on the invitations that 'Lanterns should be brought'.

GUY FAWKES NIGHT

This is also so well known an occasion that little need be said about it. In addition to the fireworks, however, the evening can be made a fuller one by arranging for the children (and the adults) to roast potatoes and chestnuts in the embers. As it is frequently cold and frosty on this evening, it is also a good plan to provide refreshments by way of hot soup, hot cocoa, and other liquids often more favoured by adults. Home-made toffee is also customary on this evening in many parts of the country.

Make certain, too, that you have your first-aid box immediately at hand and that in it you have an ample supply of burn dressings and lotion or jelly. Someone is absolutely certain to need them.

SECTION THREE
ESSENTIAL PARTY EQUIPMENT

Certain small items of equipment should be available in every house where a party is to be held. Nothing can be more disruptive to the flow and continuity of a party than to find, at the crucial moment, that there is no scribbling paper, or there aren't enough pencils to go round. It is almost inevitable, too, that when such crises arrive it is either too late to go to the shop around the corner or (equally inevitable) it is early closing day.

By the invitations sent out and the replies received, you will have an approximate idea of the number of guests who should arrive. With children's parties, the numbers are liable to be slightly less than anticipated, as colds, mumps, chicken pox, and other maladies peculiar to everybody's children other than your own are apt to play last-minute havoc with numbers.

With adult parties the numbers may well be more than anticipated, as unexpected guests (and often unwilling ones) are apt to come along in tow with the guest you hadn't really wanted to invite anyway ('Charlie popped in just as I was leaving, so I insisted he came; I said you'd be only too delighted').

The following items of small equipment are therefore suggested as being indispensable, and should be obtained well beforehand.

FOR CHILDREN'S PARTIES

Balloons One per child plus 100% reserve for use in games and to replace the ones which burst just as the child is about to leave for home. With twenty guests, have not less than forty balloons.

18

Pencils One per guest plus at least six spare ones. It is a good plan to have a special box of party pencils. This can be started off by buying a dozen or so good pencils and cutting them in half. Most modern pencil manufacturers make pencils which are very difficult to break (the lead is bonded to the wood) and will stand any amount of rough usage.

The stock of pencils can be kept up by putting in the box all household or family pencils which are less than three to four inches in length.

Pencil Sharpeners Have at least two in the box. Buy two good ones; they will not only last longer but will also sharpen the pencils more efficiently and will thus save money by reducing sharpening breakages to the minimum.

Small Scribbling Pads One per guest plus half a dozen spare. These can be obtained very cheaply at the local multiple stores, and will last for two or three parties at least.

A Supply of Paper Handkerchiefs Some child is almost certain to have forgotten or to lose his or her handkerchief. They are also useful for certain games.

A Box of Drinking Straws (preferably plastic ones). These can be used in certain games (*Blow Football*, for example), as well as for their designed purpose.

Large Safety Pins Apart from their use in certain games, these are useful for immediately preserving the dignity of some young man who sheds a button during the excitement of a more boisterous game.

Table Tennis Balls Indispensable for a number of games. Have at least half a dozen. Buy cheap ones, not the rather expensive balls used in first-class table tennis circles.

Small Balls Old tennis balls will do admirably. If you wish, a small number of perforated plastic balls, which may be thrown about a room with no fear of damage to life, limb, or your best pictures, can be bought with advantage and used solely for parties.

Items of Spare Clothing Know where you can put your hands immediately on a pair of old knickers or underpants. Accidents will happen!

Packs of Cards Have two or three packs available. They can be used for a variety of games (see Throwing Games, pages 62–74). One or more packs of 'Happy Families' are also invaluable.

First Aid Equipment This is a 'must' and should never be forgotten or neglected. Some child is almost certain to bump, bruise, or cut himself.

A Supply of Small Prizes In no circumstances should these be expensive, or the inevitable pot-hunter will be disclosed. Bars of chocolate, small packets of sweets, pencils, thimbles, and such-like items are all that are necessary. It is also advisable not to distribute prizes too freely, certainly not for every competitive game, otherwise some children will soon be competing for the prize and not for the fun of the thing.

Individual Items These may be needed for specific games you intend to introduce into your programme. Such items may include things like waste-paper baskets, bowls (for games like *Duck Apple*), string, rope, clothes pegs, and so on. It is imperative that they should be immediately at hand when required and that you or someone else should not have to go hunting for them. It is a good idea to put all these items (and the others as well) into a clothes basket so that they are all together right from the beginning of the party.

ADULT PARTIES

Most of the items enumerated above (except spare clothing) will also be required for adult parties. Gramophone records may also be needed, particularly at parties catering for teen-agers. A greater stress is liable to be placed on the individual items for special games; newspapers, sheets of brown paper, and so on are almost certain to be required. To ensure that everything is available, *write down* the games you intend to introduce and by the side of them list the items of equipment which may be needed. Get these together not later than the day before the party (you will almost certainly be much too busy with food on the day itself) and, as with children's parties, have them immediately available for use when needed.

SECTION FOUR
GAMES FOR VERY YOUNG CHILDREN

Nursery Rhyme Mimes

As most young children live almost constantly in the land of make-believe, miming actions to Nursery Rhymes are always popular and can be used as quieter games between the more boisterous ones.

Let them all stand in a circle or sit on the floor, then you or they recite some well-known rhymes whilst they do the actions. Most of them will do it almost spontaneously, but if such is not the case you can suggest various actions which can be done. Two examples are given below:

'*Pat a cake, pat a cake, baker's man*' (Clap hands or pat knees)

'*Bake me a cake as quick as you can*' (Wave hands about quickly)

'*Pat it, and prick it, and mark it with "B"*' (Pat knees, pretend to make holes in it with a pin and draw a letter 'B' in the air)

'*Put it in the oven for baby and me*' (Pretend to open the oven door, slide in the cake, and close the door)

'*Sing a song of sixpence*'

'*A pocket full of rye*' (Turn out pockets or put hands in them)

'*Four and twenty blackbirds*' (Flap arms or elbows about like wings)

'*Baked in a pie*' (Pretend to be mixing dough)

'*When the pie was opened*' (Pretend to cut open a pie and look in)

'*The birds began to sing*' (Whistle, chirrup, or sing)

21

'*Wasn't that a dainty dish*'
'*To set before a king?*' (Carry an imaginary dish and put it on the table)
'*The king was in his counting house*'
'*Counting out his money*' (Pretend to count—like a miser)
'*The maid was in the garden*'
'*Hanging out the clothes*' (Pretend to peg clothes on a line)
'*When down came a blackbird*' (A lot of wing flapping)
'*And pecked off her nose*' (Hold nose as if in obvious pain)

Other well known rhymes suitable for miming are: Little Boy Blue, Humpty Dumpty, Little Miss Muffet, Ride a Cock Horse, Little Bo Peep, Goosey Goosey Gander, Little Jack Horner, The Queen of Hearts, Ding Dong Bell, There Was an Old Woman who Lived in a Shoe, Old Mother Hubbard, Simple Simon, Georgie Porgie, etc.

You will find that the children will almost certainly want to play three or four of them at least twice each—so that's a good ten minutes gone.

Oranges and Lemons (Indoors or Outdoors)

This game is one of the most popular perennials ever. Two of the children make an arch by standing facing each other and holding hands above their heads. One agrees to be 'ORANGES' and the other 'LEMONS'.

The other children walk behind each other in a small circle continually passing under the arch. As they walk, they sing:

'Oranges and lemons,' say the bells of St Clement's,
'You owe me five farthings,' say the bells of St Martin's.
'When will you pay me?' say the bells of Old Bailey,
'When I grow rich,' say the bells of Shoreditch.
'When will that be?' say the bells of Stepney,
'I'm sure I don't know,' says the great bell of Bow.

     Here comes a candle to light you to bed,
     Here comes a chopper to chop off your head,
     Chip! chop! chip! chop!

As the last words are sung, the two children forming the arch move their arms up and down, finally bringing them well down to entrap one of the children walking through the arch. They then ask him or her which he chooses, oranges or lemons? Having chosen, say oranges, he then stands behind the child in the arch who has previously agreed to be that.

The game goes on until all the children have been caught and chosen to be an orange or a lemon.

The oranges then have a tug-of-war with the lemons.

Looby Loo (Indoors or Outdoors)

Most of the children will know the tune for this game, as it is almost certain they will have heard it on television.

As the actions are mentioned in the verses, the children do them. A circle is formed and the children sing.

> Here we go (or dance) looby loo,
> Here we go looby light.
> Here we go looby loo
> All on a Saturday night.

> Put all your right hands in
> And shake them all around.
> Take all your right hands out
> And turn yourselves about.

(Do the same with the left hand as well, then both hands.)

> Put all your right feet in
> And shake them all around
> Take all your right feet out
> And turn yourselves about.

(Repeat this verse saying 'left foot in'.)

> Put your both feet in
> And shake them all around
> Take your both feet out
> And turn yourselves about.

Finish the game by singing:

> Put your whole self in
> And shake yourself about
> Take your whole self out
> And turn yourselves about.

The children will almost certainly want to repeat it at least two or three times.

The Mulberry Bush (Indoors or Outdoors)

This is a musical miming game in which the children mime the actions they are singing about. They form a circle and sing:

> Here we go round the mulberry bush,
> The mulberry bush, the mulberry bush,
> Here we go round the mulberry bush,
> On a cold and frosty morning.

(As they sing, they all walk round in a circle.)

> This is the way we wash our clothes,
> Wash our clothes, wash our clothes,
> This is the way we wash our clothes,
> On a cold and frosty morning.

(Each child pretends to be washing clothes.)

Each child in turn can then sing the first line of a new verse, and as it is sung the actions are mimed. Some suggested first lines might be:

> This is the way we iron our clothes,
> This is the way we darn our socks,
> This is the way we brush our teeth,
> This is the way we clean our shoes,
> This is the way we walk to school,
> This is the way we comb our hair,
> This is the way we scrub the floors,
> This is the way we dance at school, etc.

Each child should have at least two or three turns at singing a fresh line. The moment they begin to run out of ideas, stop the game and start another one.

The Farmer in his Den (Indoors and Outdoors)

There are several variations of this musical game, sometimes known as *Farmer in the Dell*. Here is a simple version:

All the children form a circle round one standing in the centre. They then walk round the centre child (the farmer) singing—

> The Farmer in his den,
> The Farmer in his den,
> Heigh-ho, heigh-ho,
> The Farmer in his den.

> The Farmer wants a wife,
> The Farmer wants a wife,
> Heigh-ho, heigh-ho,
> The Farmer wants a wife.

(Here the Farmer chooses a 'wife' to stand in the circle with him.)

> The wife wants a child,
> The wife wants a child,
> Heigh-ho, heigh-ho.
> The wife wants a child.

(The Farmer's wife now chooses another child to stand in the middle.)

> The child wants a nurse,
> The child wants a nurse,
> Heigh-ho, heigh-ho,
> The child wants a nurse.

(A nurse is now chosen by the 'child' and stands in the centre.)

> The nurse wants a dog,
> The nurse wants a dog,

Heigh-ho, heigh-ho,
The nurse wants a dog.

(A dog takes his place in the centre, chosen by the 'nurse'.)

We all pat the dog,
We all pat the dog,
Heigh-ho, heigh-ho,
We all pat the dog.

Everybody playing the game then proceeds to pat the dog (reasonably gently) on the head and back for a few moments.

The game then starts all over again with the 'dog' becoming the 'Farmer'.

Children will play this game without any signs of boredom at least four or five times.

Squeak, Piggy, Squeak (4 plus to 7 plus. Indoors)

This is a great favourite with little girls of $4\frac{1}{2}$ to $7\frac{1}{2}$ years of age or thereabouts. Change the title to *Grunt, Piggy, Grunt* or *Roar, Lion, Roar,* and it becomes an equal favourite with boys of the same age.

All the players except one sit cross-legged in a circle on the carpet (or on the dry grass in summer).

The remaining player is blindfolded and placed in the centre of the circle, holding a cushion in front of her. (The cushion is for her protection.) She is led slowly round the circle and when she says 'stop' is turned to face the nearest sitting player to her. She then gently places the cushion on the knees of the sitting player, turns round, sits on it and then demands 'Squeak, Piggy, Squeak', whereon the player being sat on makes a little squeaking noise. The blindfolded player tries to guess who it is. If she is successful, she changes places with the squeaker, but if unsuccessful she gets up and adopts a similar procedure until she finally succeeds in guessing right.

The Muffin Man (Children 5 to 8. Indoors or Outdoors)

The players join hands in a circle in the centre of which is one player who is blindfolded and has a walking stick or ruler.

The players skip or dance round singing:

Have you seen the muffin man, the muffin man, the muffin man,
Have you seen the muffin man who lives in Drury Lane?

At the words 'Drury Lane' they all stand still whilst the centre player points his stick or ruler at someone in the circle. Whoever is in line with the pointer moves forward and grasps the stick. The centre player then asks three questions—any questions will do, but they should require only one-word answers. 'Are you enjoying yourself?' or 'What kind of jelly do you like best?' The player answers the questions in a disguised voice, and the Muffin Man is then allowed three guesses as to the identity of the player holding the stick. If he guesses correctly, he joins the outside circle and the other player becomes the Muffin Man. If his guess is incorrect the game continues as before.

Ring a Ring o' Roses (Indoors or Outdoors on a lawn)

The children join hands to make a circle and walk or dance round and round singing:

> Ring a ring o' Roses,
> A pocketful of posies,
> Atishoo! atishoo!
> We all fall down.

As the word 'down' is sung, still with hands joined, they all drop to sit cross-legged on the floor.

Even a simple game like this can be good fun for at least five minutes.

Three Blind Mice (Indoors or Outdoors. Plenty of room needed)

The children join hands to form a circle round 'The Farmer's Wife', who can be a child or an adult.

They walk or skip round singing the nursery rhyme,

> Three blind mice, see how they run, etc.

as the word 'mice' is sung in the last line they all dash for the sides of the room or lawn to avoid being tagged by the Farmer's Wife. The first one to be tagged becomes the Farmer's Wife in turn.

Pussy Wants a Corner (Indoors or Outdoors)

All the children except one who is 'Pussy' stand in corners of the room or at spots decided upon, if there are a large number of children.

Pussy goes from one child to another saying, 'Please let me come in your corner' or 'Pussy wants your corner'. They all refuse, but as Pussy moves about or talks to a child in a corner, children in other corners try to change places with each other. Pussy (who must be very alert) tries to get into one of the empty corners as a change-over is being made. If she succeeds, the one left without a corner becomes 'Pussy'.

The Wind and the Flowers (5 plus to 8 plus. Outdoors or in a fairly large room)

The players are divided into two equal groups, the 'wind' and the 'flowers', who stand behind a line at each end of the playing space. The 'flowers' decide amongst themselves the name of one common flower such as daisy, buttercup, dandelion, etc., and then stand in line facing and a few yards from the 'wind'.

The 'wind' group try to guess the name of the flower selected and call out the names of flowers. Immediately the right one, *ie* the one selected by the 'flower' group, is called, the 'flowers' dash for the safety of their 'home' chased by the 'wind'. Any 'flowers' which are tagged become part of the 'wind' and help to chase. The game continues for a set time, or until all the 'flowers' have been caught. Then the roles are reversed, the 'flowers' take a turn at being the 'wind' and vice versa.

What Is the Time, Mr Wolf? (Indoors or Outdoors)

One child is Mr Wolf. He walks about and all the children follow him. One after another they call out, 'What is the time,

28

Mr Wolf?' So long as he says any time except 'Twelve o'clock —Dinner time' everyone is safe, but the moment he says that everyone dashes for safety—which can be the sides of the room or the edge of the lawn. Anyone tagged before reaching safety becomes 'Mr Wolf'.

Hill Dill (6 plus to 10 plus. Indoors or Outdoors; large room, lawn, or beach)

The playing area is divided into three parts by lines on the ground, or by ropes laid flat on the floor.

Two teams of about equal size are formed; these stand in the two outside parts, one in each, whilst a single player stands in the centre part.

When the player in the centre shouts out 'Hill Dill, come over the Hill' the groups in the end spaces change places. The centre player tries to tag as many as possible; those he does join him in the centre to help him tag the others as they cross over. The child who remains untagged the longest is the winner.

The Witch's Ring (girls or boys 6 to 8 plus. Outdoors or large room indoors)

In the centre of the room or lawn is placed a mat or hoop, on which the 'Witch' crouches down. All the other players walk round her in a circle singing nursery rhymes or popular songs.

Very slowly the witch begins to stand up. When she is at full height she suddenly shouts, 'Here I come', and then chases the other players until she has tagged four or five. As each one is tagged, the witch turns her into some object which can be mimed, say a tree with its branches blowing about in a gale, a caterpillar, a windmill, and so on. The last person to be caught becomes the witch.

Suspense can be added if the witch varies her rate of rising, or even sinks down again once or twice before reaching full height.

Squirrels in the Trees (6 to 9. Large room or lawn)

The children stand in pairs, face to face with hands joined to represent hollow trees. In each hollow tree stands a third player who is the squirrel. The trees with their squirrels should be spaced unevenly about the room.

One extra player is a squirrel without a tree.

When he or she either claps her hands or calls 'change' all the squirrels hunt for a new tree. The homeless squirrel also tries to find a home during the general change over. Whoever does not succeed in finding a home then becomes the one to clap or call 'change'.

Busy Bee (6 plus to 8 plus. Indoors or Outdoors)

Each child chooses a partner, and the pairs space themselves out over the playing area. The leader (or you) calls out various commands such as 'stand side to side' or 'back to back' or 'link elbows'. However, when the leader calls out 'busy bee' each player tries to find a new partner; the leader also tries, and if successful the unlucky one left out becomes the leader and gives the commands.

Jack in the Box (6 plus to 8 plus. Large room or lawn)

At one end of the room or lawn place a mat or hoop on or in which stands 'Jack'. The rest of the players stand in a space at

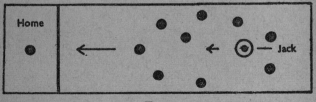

Fig 2

the other end. This can be marked off with a piece of string or rope (*see* Fig 2). To start, all the players (except Jack) stand in the 'home'. They then walk round and round Jack in his box, singing or saying, 'Jack in the Box, come out and play, catch us now or we'll run away'. Without warning, Jack jumps as high as he can out of his box and tries to tag as many as he can before they reach 'home'. Those tagged drop out. The winner is the last person to be tagged; he or she then becomes 'Jack'.

The Hunter and the Rabbits (6 plus to 8 plus. Large room or lawn)

This is a similar type of game to Jack in the Box. The space is divided identically and a mat or hoop is placed on the ground as a 'house' for the hunter.

The 'rabbits' come out of their 'burrows' and walk around the field. When the hunter leaves his house, all the 'rabbits' run behind him and crouch, jump, or 'bunny-hop' in line. When the hunter turns round the 'rabbits' try to keep out of his sight. When he stops, turns round very quickly, and claps his hands, the 'rabbits' try to scoot back to their burrows without being tagged.

Hunt the Slipper (4 plus to 7 plus. Indoors or Outdoors)

The children sit in a tight circle with one standing or sitting in the centre. He is given a slipper or a shoe which he hands to one of the players in the circle. He (or all the children) recites out loud:

> Cobbler, cobbler mend my shoe,
> Have it done by half past two.

The centre player then closes his eyes and puts his hands over them. As he does so everyone chants.

> Cobbler, cobbler, tell me true,
> Which of you has got my shoe?

As this chant is going on the children pass the slipper round the circle behind their backs, and whoever is holding it when the last word 'shoe' is said, retains it, holding it out of sight.

The centre player then opens his eyes and by looking round the circle at the expressions on the children's faces tries to guess who is holding the shoe. If he does not guess correctly in two tries the one who is holding the slipper takes his place in the centre.

If he does guess correctly he is allowed one more turn as the centre player—but not more.

Donkey's Tail (6 to any age)

You need a small blackboard, or a piece of hardboard about two feet by eighteen inches plus a piece of string with a drawing pin through one end for this old favourite.

On the blackboard or hardboard draw an 'animal' (without a tail) as large as possible in chalk and mark with a small dot the place where the tail would grow from, like this:

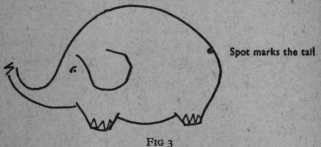

Spot marks the tail

FIG 3

Prop your work of art up on a chair or other suitable place. Each competitor in turn is given the piece of string with the drawing pin in one end and is then placed about six feet away (or two steps) from the 'animal', where he is either blindfolded or told to close his eyes.

He then steps forward and tries to pin the tail to the exact spot marked on the drawing. (You will find it amazing how many animals develop tails on their ears or under their stomachs!) The one who puts the tail nearest to the correct spot wins the contest. It is advisable to initial the mark made by each competitor so that later there can be no arguments as to who made which mark.

Poor Puss-cat (for the younger children, 5 plus to 8 plus but can be used effectively with mixed teenagers)

All sit on chairs or on the floor in a circle. One player then goes into the centre to become the poor puss-cat. The cat, on hands and knees making cat noises and purring loudly, goes to each person in turn, who must keep a perfectly solemn face, stroke the cat on the head or back and say, 'Poor pussy, poor puss-cat'. Anyone who smiles or laughs whilst stroking and talking to the cat must take its place in the centre of the circle.

Make a Rhyme (6 plus to 8 plus. Indoors or Outdoors)

Another quiet sitting-down game for younger children.

One player stands up and says, 'I want a rhyme in jolly quick time and the word I choose is Ben'.

Each child in turn then has to give a word which rhymes with Ben, *eg* pen, hen, den, men, ten, and so on.

Any player who cannot answer in, say, ten seconds, loses a 'life'. At the end of the game, when each player has asked for a rhyme, the one who has lost the least number of lives is the winner.

It is a good plan to insist that each questioner must know at least five words which rhyme with the one he or she chooses. This will prevent hold-ups and will also stop unrhymable words such as SILVER and ORANGE being chosen.

Sound and Action (4 plus to 8 plus. Indoors or Outdoors)

A game for younger children. All sit in a circle or semi-circle. One then gets up, faces the rest, and starts to make up a story about birds and animals.

Whenever a bird is mentioned, those sitting down stand up and flap their arms like wings five times and then sit down again; whenever an animal is mentioned they remain seated but try to make a noise like the one made by the animal mentioned. A story might begin like this: 'One day when I was in the country, I saw a dog' (all remain seated but bark) 'who was barking at a cat' (all remain seated but make cat noises) 'which had climbed a tree to try to catch a blackbird' (all stand and flap five times) . . .

Any player who does not do the correct movement or who does not make the correct noise, or who is slow in doing the right thing, drops out of the game. The winner is the one who remains longest.

SECTION FIVE

INTRODUCING GAMES

Know Your Neighbour (teenagers upwards)

This is an 'introducing game' which can be made into a competition. Make some small labels (half a postcard will do) and write on each a number, *eg* if there are twelve guests, numbers from 1–12 will be required. It will help your preliminary organisation if you give odd numbers to the boys and even numbers to the girls.

As the guests arrive, each one is given a number which they pin on themselves and a sheet of paper on which six tasks are written; the tasks for the boys will involve them talking with all the girls in turn, and vice versa.

When all are present each player sets about completing his or her lists of tasks as quickly as possible, the first boy and girl to do so being the winner. Here are some suggestions:

Questions for the boys to ask

(1) Ask No 2 the names of the last four films she has seen.
(2) Ask No 4 where she has spent her last four holidays.
(3) Ask No 6 the names of the last four books she has read.
(4) Ask No 8 the names of her four favourite film stars.
(5) Ask No 10 what are the four things she likes best of all.
(6) Ask No 12 her four greatest dislikes.

Questions for the girls to ask

(1) Ask No 1 who are his four favourite sportsmen.
(2) Ask No 3 the names of four places he wouldn't like to go on holiday.

(3) Ask No 5 the names of four brands of cigarettes he likes.

(4) Ask No 5 the four things he likes best of all for dinner.

(5) Ask No 7 the names of his four favourite sports-women.

(6) Ask No 9 the names of his four favourite crime writers.

(7) Ask No 11 the names of four famous detectives in fiction.

As an alternative to the above type of question, tasks such as given below can be set.

(1) Introduce No 3 to Nos 6, 8, and 10.

(2) Introduce yourself to No 5 and help him to choose three girls whom he would like best to take to the cinema.

(3) Find No 4, introduce her to No 5, and get them involved in a discussion about dance music.

(4) See if you can find anyone who is really interested in Ballet and Opera and get them to tell you why.

If the above type of task is given, the game will be non-competitive but will achieve the aim of making your guests talk amongst themselves.

Name the Advert (11 plus and Adults. Indoors)

This is a useful 'introducing game' at the beginning of a party. Beforehand, paste on to a large sheet of paper about twenty advertisements of nationally known articles which can be cut from newspapers or magazines, but *cut out the name of the article*. Number the advertisements from 1 to 20.

Provide every guest with paper and pencil and ask them to study the advertisements and then write down on their papers what they think the advertised articles to be. All the guests are allowed to discuss the advertisements with the others. (They will do, in any case.)

A small prize should be given to the one who produces a complete list when called upon. At least fifteen minutes can be allowed for this game—more if you make a few of the items

Spill the Beans (Teenagers and upwards)

As each guest arrives, he or she is given five beans (dried peas or matches will serve equally well) and told that the object of the game is to talk to someone and try to make them say 'Yes' or 'No' by asking questions, or by any other means they can think of.

If successful, they hand over a bean to the unfortunate one who has said 'Yes' or 'No', and move on to someone else.

The first person to get rid of all of his or her beans is the winner.

Junior Paul Jones (6 plus to 10 plus)

Younger children rarely require 'mixing' games to get to know each other, as most of them are spontaneously friendly. However, this is a simple 'mixer' which might be useful on the odd occasion.

Two concentric circles are formed facing each other, boys in one circle, girls in the other. When the music plays they run or skip round in opposite directions; when it stops they are told to do certain actions with the boy or girl opposite, such as 'Join hands and spin round five times', 'Shake hands with each other, five times with each hand and five times with both', 'Each of you hum a song and ask your partner to guess what it is', 'Find out your partner's name, age, address, and school', 'Girls try to do an Irish Jig and boys a Sailor's Hornpipe'.

Who Am I? (Teenagers and upwards)

A little previous preparation is needed for this 'mixer'.

On half postcards write down the names of famous characters (one name on each card) and fix a safety pin to a corner of the card.

When the guests arrive, one of the cards is pinned on the back of each. They then have to ask questions of each other, to try to find the identity of the person on the card. As soon as anyone does this, the card is pinned on the front of his clothing.

39

It is also useful to number the cards, and arrange that for the first game, No 1 pairs with No 2, No 3 with No 4 and so on.

Suitable names to write on the cards are famous characters of history and fiction, film and television stars, sportsmen and sportswomen, etc.

New Angles

Make about ten small drawings of common objects seen from an unusual view point; some examples are given in Fig 4.

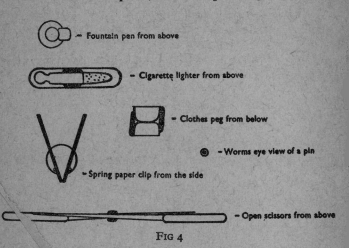

FIG 4

As the guests arrive, give each of them a pencil and paper and ask them to study the drawings and to write down what they think the objects to be. Tell them to discuss them with the other guests and get their views as well.

MUSICAL GAMES

Musical Bumps (4 to 7 plus. Indoors)

All the players form a circle. Whilst the music plays, they bob up and down doing little skip jumps. The moment the music stops everyone flops down on to the floor and sits cross legged. The last one down is eliminated. Continue till only one is left.

Musical Mats (6 to 10 plus. Indoors or Outdoors)

Place four or five newspapers (or mats) unequally spaced around the room (or lawn). All the players form a large circle, and when the music starts they walk, trip, or skip round the room, always stepping on the 'mats' as they pass them. When the music stops, anyone actually on a mat, even with only one foot, drops out of the game. As the numbers get smaller, the mats should be brought in closer together.

Musical Islands (6 to 10 plus. Indoors or Outdoors)

This is similar in style to *Musical Mats*. Papers or mats are placed about the room or lawn. As the music plays, the players walk or skip about, but when it stops they must stand with both feet on one of the 'islands'. Not more than two players are allowed on any one island. Anyone not finding an island is eliminated. Remove one or two islands after each stop.

Patterns (8 plus to 12 plus. Large room or lawn)

No apparatus is required for this time-passing game. The children arrange themselves into teams of six to eight. When the music starts, they walk about quite freely. As they are walking, the leader calls out a letter or shape, say a square or an 'E'. The moment the music stops, each team rushes to form the shape called out. The team that makes the best shape first is awarded a point. At the end of the game the team that

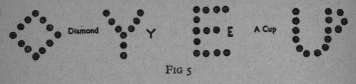

FIG 5

has the most points is the winner. Some suggestions on shapes are shown in Fig 5.

Musical Rush (6 to 10 plus. Outdoors or in large room)

The players in this game should preferably be all the same sex and about the same age. In the centre of the space available place a number of small objects, *eg* corks, cotton reels, marbles, pebbles, etc. The number of objects should always be at least one less than the number of players. All the players skip round the outside edge of the playing space whilst the music is playing, but the moment it stops they all rush to pick up one of the objects. Anyone failing to do so drops out.

Musical Arches (6 to 10 plus. Indoors or Outdoors)

This is a musical game in which everyone takes part right until the end. Two pairs of children stand, one at each side of the room or lawn, joining hands overhead to make an arch. The remainder of the children in pairs line up round the room all facing one way. When the music begins they walk or skip round the room and pass under the two arches. When the music stops, any pair caught under the arches form arches in turn. The game continues until all have been caught except one pair of children; these are the winners.

Nursery Rhymes (6 to 10 plus or older. Indoors or Outdoors)

This is a singing game for younger children who are divided into two groups sitting on opposite sides of the room.

One side starts by singing any nursery rhyme, say 'Little Jack Horner'. Whilst they are singing this, the other side thinks of another rhyme, and the moment the first side has finished, the second one must start.

This goes on until one side fails to find another rhyme to sing, or starts to sing one which has already been used by themselves or the opposite side.

It is useful for each side to have a leader who calls out to his side the title of the next rhyme, though anyone in the team is allowed to suggest rhymes to the leader.

Musical Grab (6 to 10 plus. Outdoors or in a large room)

This is a team game requiring one book or similar small object per team. These objects are placed on a cushion or mat or newspaper situated equidistant from the teams. If there are two teams they would face each other as shown in Fig 6a. Three teams would be as in 6b, and four teams in a square 6c.

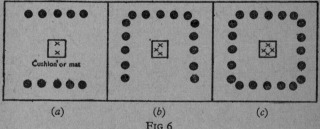

(a)   (b)   (c)

FIG 6

As the music plays, one player from the end of the line runs to the mat, grabs an object, and takes it back to his team, handing it on to the next player, who takes it back to the cushion. The third player collects it and hands it to the fourth, and so on.

Any person actually holding an object when the music stops is eliminated. After, say, five minutes play, the team with the greatest number of players still remaining in the game is the winner.

Musical Numbers (Any age from 6 upwards. Indoors or Outdoors)

All the players walk or skip round the room as the music plays. When the music stops they rush to form circles or groups of a number given out whilst the music is playing, *eg* when the music is playing the leader or hostess calls out 'fives'. The moment the music stops the players form groups of five. Anyone unable to find a place drops out. The leader should count the players to ensure that someone must be eliminated. If there are ten players, for example, he can call 'eights', 'fours', or 'sixes', but not 'fives'.

Musical Parcel (6 plus to any age)

Place a small present in a little box and then wrap it in seven or eight layers of paper, each layer being tied up with a number of pieces of string.

All the players sit round in a circle and the parcel is given to one of them to untie the knots and unwrap the parcel. As this is being done, the music plays. (Whoever is responsible for the music should not be able to see the players.) The music is stopped at frequent intervals, and the instant this happens, the parcel is passed to the next player in the circle. Whoever succeeds in finally opening the box and taking out the present *while the music is playing* is the winner and receives the present.

Musical Race (8 plus to any age. Indoors or Outdoors)

Another variation of *Musical Chairs*. The chairs are arranged in a circle facing outwards. There must be one chair for each player and *not* less as in the case of *Musical Chairs*.

The players sit on their chairs and carefully note their position, who they are next to, what they are opposite, and so on.

When the music starts they all walk clockwise round the circle of chairs, but the moment it stops, each one dashes to get to his chair, the last one to sit down being eliminated. (Strict umpiring may be necessary.)

It is most important that *no one must run back* to his chair, even if it has only just been passed, but must go forward right round the circle.

As distinct from *Musical Chairs*, there is no need to take away a chair after each stoppage of the music, the whole original circle can remain until all except one of the players are eliminated.

GAMES WITH BALLOONS

Balloon Blow (6 plus to any age. Indoors)

Small teams of about four or five players are needed, plus one circular balloon for each team. The leaders throw up their balloons at the starting signal, and then all the teams try to keep their balloons in the air by blowing at them. The hands or other parts of the body must not touch the balloon. The team that keeps its balloon up the longest is the winner.

Pushing the Pig

This is a race for teams of four or five players. One sausage-shaped balloon and one walking stick or umbrella per team is required.

Teams stand behind a line or a stick or piece of string laid on the ground. About ten to fifteen feet in front of the teams is a second line.

The first player in each team places his balloon or pig on the floor by his feet and holds the stick in his hand. On the signal to start he proceeds to push or prod his balloon forwards (the prodding must be done only at the ends of the balloon—not in its middle) over the far line and back to the starting line, where he then hands the stick to the second player to do likewise.

The second player hands over to the third and so on until each member of the team has completed the course. The first team so to do is the winner.

Balloon Blowing Race

A course similar to that for *Pushing the Pig* is required, along with one round balloon per team and one drinking straw per player.

On this relay the balloon is blown over the course, the blowing being done through the drinking straw. Alternative methods of blowing are by mouth alone or by bicycle pumps, if such are available.

Balloon Tapping Relay

One balloon and one ruler, short cane, or stick are required for each team. Competitors again cover a short course tapping the balloon upwards and forwards and handing on the ruler to the next in the team.

Balloon Heading Relay

A game more suitable for boys of eleven years and over. Normal relay procedure over a short course with the balloon being headed by each competitor. If possible, have the teams fairly widely spaced apart to minimise the risk of the players bumping heads.

Balloon Overhead Relay

A simple passing race involving a minimum of running and requiring one balloon per team.

Teams stand in line, each member of the team standing close behind the one in front.

The leader holds the balloon. On the starting signal the balloon is passed overhead down the team to the last player, who, on receiving it, runs to the front of the team and continues the overhead passing. This goes on until the original leader has received the balloon at the back of the team and then returns to the front and holds the balloon high above his head.

An alternative method of passing, more suitable for boys, is underneath the legs—or alternately over the head and under the legs—*ie* the first player passes it overhead, the second under the legs, and so on.

Charlie Chaplin Relay

This activity is suitable for children of eight or nine years of age upwards, teenagers, and adults. One balloon, one book,

47

one walking stick per team, plus a fair amount of room are required; a lawn would be suitable.

A short course of about twenty feet in length is required. Normal relay procedure is used; each player in the team covering the course and handing over to the next player.

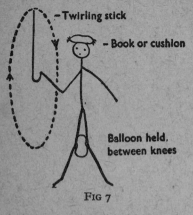

- Twirling stick
- Book or cushion

Balloon held between knees

FIG 7

The balloon is held between the knees, the book balanced on the head (a small cushion would also be suitable), and the cane or stick twirled *à la* Charles Chaplin (*see* Fig 7). If the balloon is released from between the knees or the book is dropped from the head it must be picked up and replaced by the competitor before continuing the course.

Circle Balloon Race

Teams form circles. These should be of the same size; this can be done, if conditions permit, by drawing circles on the floor, or by making the competitors link arms, or grasp outstretched hands and then release their grips.

The leader of each team holds the balloon in both hands. On the signal to start, the balloon is passed from hand to hand round the circle of players a given number of times, say three. The first team to do this is the winner. An alternative is to pass the balloon behind the backs. If the balloon is dropped it must be retrieved by the one who dropped it and the passing continued.

Balloon Tap-up Race

A circle formation is required for this team race as for *Circle Balloon Race*. Instead of the balloon being passed directly

48

from one player to the other, each person taps it upwards with one hand to at least head height a given number of times (three or four) and then taps it to the next player, who does likewise. With this race two circuits of the circle is quite sufficient, and with young players one will be enough.

Ten Trips

Players are arranged in threes who stand in line about four feet apart from each other. On the starting signal each three try to make ten trips of the balloon by tapping it with one hand

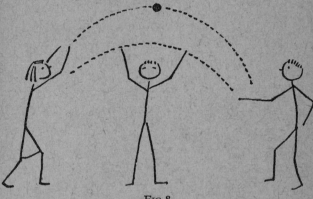

FIG 8

from one to the other as shown in Fig 8 in the shortest possible time. The first three to complete the ten trips are the winners.

With younger children, five or six trips are quite sufficient. This activity can be done out of doors in summer using a tennis or small rubber ball, the players can then stand farther apart.

Outdoor Balloon Ball

An ideal team game for boys which can be played in a fairly large room or better still on a lawn or the beach. A pitch forty to fifty feet long by about twenty feet wide would be ideal. In

49

the middle of each end line make a goal about eight to ten feet wide. This can be marked with canes (long ones) or even caps or pebbles.

The object of the game is to score goals.

The following rules are suggested in the interests of safety, but these can be modified to suit local conditions and the exuberance or otherwise of the players:

(1) The balloon must be struck with a flat hand only, no clenched fists.

(2) There must be no intentional pushing, shoving, barging, kicking, or rough play of any kind.

(3) Goals can be scored only if the balloon passes through the goal at below waist height.

(4) The balloon must never be caught and held; it can, however, be dribbled forwards by pat bouncing it on the hand.

(5) Play can be of any duration, but five or six minutes each way is suggested as being quite sufficient.

(6) If the balloon goes out of play over the side lines it is tapped in by a player of the opposite side from the one who last touched it before going out of play.

(7) To start the game, the referee taps the balloon in the air between two centre players. After a goal has been scored there is no centre tap-off, the balloon being tapped straight into play by the unfortunate goalkeeper.

Indoor Balloon Ball

This game can be played in almost any normal sized room by players of any age, by both sexes and by mixed teams of children and adults. There is no running about; in fact, everyone, by rule, must be seated all the time. Two equal teams of five or six players (or less), one chair or stool per player, and one balloon are required (Fig 9).

Arrange two rows of chairs (one for each member of the teams) about two short paces apart. The teams sit facing one another. Each team then tries to tap the balloon over the heads of the opposing team *so that it falls to the ground behind them.*

It is advisable not to have a hanging light between the opposing teams!

FIG 9

The rules are simple:

(1) The balloon must always be struck with an open hand; clenched fists or feet must not be used.

(2) A coin is tossed to determine which side shall have first strike.

(3) At all times during the game all the players must be seated. Penalties can be devised for infringement of this rule, such as giving half a point to the opposing side or removing the offender for a period of one or two minutes.

(4) The game can consist of two halves of not more than four or five minutes each.

Fanning the Balloon

Another simple relay race. One folded newspaper and one balloon per team are required. Each player fans the balloon over the set course with the folded newspaper. The balloon must not, in any circumstances, be *touched* with the paper.

An alternative form of this race is for each competitor to

sweep the balloon over the course with a large broom. The first race is perhaps the better one, because it is usually easier to obtain three or four newspapers than the same number of large brooms.

Balloon Throwing Competition

An infuriating competitive activity for any number of players, requiring little space and only one balloon.

Standing behind a line, each player tries to throw the balloon as far forwards as possible. The spot at which it touches the ground is marked by a matchstick or a piece of card with the thrower's initials written on it. Do give a small prize to the winner.

The game can be made even more infuriating for the performer and amusing for the onlooker if sausage-shaped balloons instead of circular ones are used.

Balloon Bursting Competition

Provide each competitor with an uninflated balloon which he places in his mouth ready to blow up.

He, or she, must then blow it up until it bursts. One can stipulate, to make things more difficult, that one hand or *both* hands should be clasped behind the back.

The first one to burst his balloon—blowing according to rule—is the winner. From the spectators' and the competitors' point of view, the delight of this activity is in watching the others' agonised expressions just before a balloon is due to burst.

TAGGING AND CHASING GAMES

French Tag (5 plus to 10 plus. Indoors, large room; lawn or
  beach)

The chaser tries to touch one of the other players on an
awkward part of the body, such as the knee, ankle, or foot.
Wherever the one who is tagged is touched, a hand must be
kept constantly on it until he, or she, in turn tags another
player.

Hopping the Tag (5 plus to 10 plus. Indoors or Outdoors;
  large room, lawn, or beach)

As the title implies, all movement by the players, chaser or
chased, is done by means of hopping on one leg. Legs, however, can be changed at will. When a player is not being
chased he is allowed to stand on both feet for a rest.

Walking Tag (5 plus to 10 plus. Outdoors)

This is a useful tag variation when conditions are a little
crowded. All moves must be by walking; there must be no
running about whatsoever.

Pairs Tag (5 plus to 10 plus. Indoors or Outdoors)

Two players join hands and try to tag the other players. If
they succeed in tagging one player, a chain of three is formed,
but the moment they tag another one, the four split up into
two pairs. The last person to be tagged is the winner.

All Fours Tag (5 plus to 10 plus. Indoors or Outdoors)

As the title implies, all movement is made on all fours (hands and feet); when not being chased, a player may stand up or sit down to rest.

Double Jump or Bunny-hop Tag (5 plus to 10 plus. Indoors or Outdoors)

All movement by the players must be made by jumping off both feet, which should be kept together.

Bent-knees Tag (8 plus to 12 plus. Indoors or Outdoors)

All movements must be made with the knees in the full-bend position. Players are, however, allowed to stand up when not being chased. This is an extremely strenuous activity, and should be played for only a few minutes at a time.

Chain-tag (6 plus to 10 plus. Indoors in a large room or Outdoors on a lawn or beach)

At the start of the game, two players join hands as in *Pairs Tag* (above) and try to tag the other players. As tags are made, a gradually increasing 'chain' is made until all are caught except one, who is the winner.

Cross Tag (8 plus to 12 plus. Indoors or Outdoors)

The chaser runs after, and tries to tag, another player, but if any one of the other players runs between the chaser and the one being chased, the one who has crossed between becomes the one to be chased.

Shadow Tag (5 plus to 10 plus. Outdoors on a summer's day when the sun is shining)

One player is chosen as 'he'. He tries to tag the other players, not by touching them but by stepping on their shadows.

Fox and Geese (5 plus to 10 plus. Large room, lawn, or beach)

Groups of five or six players are required for this active game. One player represents the fox, the rest Mother Goose and her young ones. Mother Goose stands with her arms held out sideways, her young ones form a line behind her holding each other round the waist. The 'fox' tries to catch the back 'gosling', but Mother Goose turns from side to side with her goslings behind her to stop this happening. The grip round the waist must not be broken.

Snake's Tail (5 plus to 10 plus. Large room, lawn, or beach)

One or more groups of five or six children required. The groups form lines holding each other round the waist. The front player in the group, *ie* the 'head' of the snake, tries to twist round and tag the back player, the 'tail'.

Hot Ball (6 plus to 10 plus)

One fairly large rubber ball required. All the players except one form a circle facing inwards and pass the ball round the circle from hand to hand. The remaining player runs round the outside of the circle trying to tag the ball. If he succeeds, whoever was holding the ball at the time tries to do the tagging, the original player taking his place in the circle.

Circle Tag Ball (8 plus to 10 plus. Indoors or Outdoors)

A large rubber ball is required. All the players except one form a circle facing inwards. If the space permits, the children should be four or five feet apart from each other. The remaining player stands in the centre of the circle. The players throw the ball to each other across the circle, whilst the centre player tries to tag it as it is thrown. If a successful tag is made the thrower changes places with the centre player.

Circle Number Tag (6 plus to 12 plus. Large room, lawn, or beach)

All the players stand in a circle with hands joined and number off by threes, fours, or fives, according to the number playing (Fig 10). The leader then calls out a number, say 'three'. Immediately all the threes in the circle chase each other in a clockwise direction round the outside of the circle; each one trying to get back to his original place without being tagged by the one behind. Each number should be called the

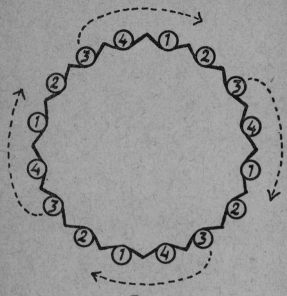

FIG 10

same number of times, and at the end of the game the player who has scored the highest number of tags is the winner.

Tag Bounce Ball (8 plus to 11 plus. Outdoors or in a large room)

One fairly large rubber ball is required. All the players except two spread themselves out over the playing area. They then pass the ball amongst themselves, but the ball must always be bounced before the pass is made. The two other players attempt to tag the ball. Players who are doing the passing may move about quite freely *if they are not actually in possession*

gether off both feet, the 'cox' helping by calling out the rhythm so that they all move in unison. 'Boats' race against each other over short distances. During the race, any 'boat' which 'breaks', *ie* anyone losing grip on the shoulders, is considered to have sunk and is disqualified.

Duck Race (5 plus to 12 plus. Large room, lawn, or beach)

This is almost identical with *Boat Race*. Groups form up in a similar manner, but instead of hopping forwards they walk forwards in the knees-full-bend position. The Leader helps the rhythm by calling out 'left–right–left' to keep them all in step.

Dragging the Ball (6 plus to any age. Indoors or Outdoors)

An exciting little team race requiring a fairly large rubber ball and a skipping rope or a piece of clothes line per team.

FIG 21

The object of the race is for each member of the team to drag a ball over a short there-and-back course by means of the rope as shown in Fig 21. This race is particularly suitable for a lawn, where the slight unevenness of the grass makes the ball more difficult to pull along.

Chin-chin or Adam's Apple (8 plus to any age)

This team passing game is particularly suitable for teenagers, but it can be played with equal amusement by both children and adults.

Teams form lines; where possible have girls and boys alternately so that a boy passes to a girl, and vice versa.

FIG 22

Now present the Leader of each team with a large apple or orange, and inform them that at the word 'go' the apple has to be passed to the end of the team and back without the hands being used at all—in fact, it must be passed from chin to chin.

The Leader is allowed to place the apple in position with his hands, the position being on the shoulder, with the chin pressing firmly on the apple. (*See* Fig 22.)

From then onwards it is chin to chin!

There is only one other rule. If the apple drops to the ground during the contest (as it inevitably will) the passer must pick it up and not the receiver.

Spoon Ball

This is a variation of *Chin-chin*. Teams are arranged as before, but one spoon per player and one table-tennis ball or marble per team is needed.

The Leader, holding the spoon handle in his mouth, places the ball in the bowl of the spoon, turns round and passes the ball to the next in line, and so on (*see* Fig 23).

If the ball is dropped (it will be), it must not be picked up by hand but by the spoon *still held in the mouth*.

Ping pong ball in a spoon

FIG 23

Nosey

This is yet another *Adam's Apple* type contest—suitable for all ages, but one in which anyone with a cold should definitely not take part!

Mixed teams are arranged in line and the outside cover of an ordinary matchbox presented to the Leaders.

They are then requested to fix this cover on their noses and to see that it is passed from nose to nose (no hands allowed again) down the team and back (*see* Fig 24).

Match box cover

FIG 24

Like the two previous games, this passing can take quite a time, so it is advisable not to have teams of more than five or six players.

A-tissue (7 plus to any age)

A team race for players of almost any age from seven to seventy. A piece of tissue paper about six inches square per

FIG 25

team is required together with one drinking straw for every player.

Each team arranges itself either in a line or in a circle. The team Leader places the tissue paper over the end of his straw, one end of which is in his mouth, and draws in his breath, causing the tissue paper to stick to the end of the straw (*see* Fig 25). He then turns to the next player and passes the paper on to him, the secret of passing being that he must exhale gently as the receiver inhales. In an identical manner the paper is passed all along the team, the first team to finish being the winner.

At no time during passing must the paper be touched by hand. If, however, it is dropped, the one who allowed it to fall is permitted to pick it up by hand and place it back in position on *his own* straw.

Nosey Parker Race (6 plus to any age. Indoors or Outdoors)

Some empty matchboxes are required. This can be either a team race or one between pairs. A short there-and-back course is decided upon, and couples line up on the start line. The two members of each pair face each other and support a matchbox cover between them by their noses. Keeping the matchbox in position and not touching it with the hands (except to pick it up and replace it, should it be dropped) they race to the end line or mark and back to the start. Because of having to keep the matchbox in position, they will be compelled to run sideways.

If the competition is run as a team race the members can split up into pairs, handing over the matchbox to the next pair on return, or the first and second can go together, then the second and third, third and fourth, and so on.

Tiddlywink Relay (Any age from 5 plus upwards. Indoors)

Normal relay procedure. One large and one small tiddlywink per team is required and one cup or tumbler.

Place the cup or tumbler about ten to fifteen feet in front of the starting line for each team, the distance being the same for all the teams.

Each Leader places his small tiddlywink on the starting line. At the signal to start he flicks it along (as in normal tiddlywinks) and tries to get it into the cup or tumbler. When he succeeds, he picks it out, dashes back to his team, places it on the start line, and gives the large 'flicker' to the second player, who repeats the whole procedure, passing it on to the third, and so on. The winning team is the one whose members complete the course first.

Pancake Race (8 plus to any age. Indoors or Outdoors)

A team relay race particularly suitable for a Shrove Tuesday party, requiring one table-tennis bat per team competing and one 'pancake' per team. The 'pancake' can be a small circular rubber or plastic mat or can be cut out of felt or other quite thick material. The Leader of each team starts off carrying the

FIG 26

bat horizontally with the pancake resting on it. At a point half way on the outward journey (which should be at least twelve to fifteen feet, more if possible) stand two other guests holding a piece of rope between them as high as possible (Fig 26). The Leader is required to toss his pancake over the rope and catch it on his bat before proceeding. If he fails the first time he must try again until he succeeds in catching it. Having done this, he goes on to the end of the outward course, where two more guests are standing holding a second rope in a similar manner to the first. The pancake is tossed over this rope and caught. Then (as you decide) the Leader can run straight back to his team and pass on the bat and pancake to the second

93

player, who repeats the same procedure. This is done by each member of the team; the first team to finish is the winner.

As an alternative to running straight back, the pancake can be tossed over both ropes again on the return journey.

To avoid making each race too long-drawn out, try not to have teams consisting of more than five or six players.

Do This, Do That (8 plus to any age)

This game is highly popular with children, but can prove amusing also to teenagers and adults. The players space themselves out quite freely in front of a Leader.

Whenever he says 'Do this' and performs some action, such as stretching his arms upwards or clapping his hands, all the players must instantly copy him. If, on the other hand, he performs an action and at the same time says 'Do that' the players must ignore the command and continue doing what they were told to do when the order 'Do this' was given.

Anyone who makes a mistake is eliminated. Similarly, if a player does not move quickly enough when 'Do this' is said he or she is eliminated also. The Leader should give the orders in fairly rapid succession, and the movements should be simple ones. The game continues until all but one are eliminated; the last person 'in' being the winner.

A variation of this one for very young children is the next game, an old favourite—

O'Grady

If the command 'O'Grady says clap your hands' is given, the action is performed, but if the Leader merely says 'Clap your hands' the children should ignore the order.

Quite Contrary (6 plus to 12 plus. Indoors or Outdoors)

This is an 'active' game, but one which does not involve the children tearing about all over the place; it is also, like *Do This, Do That* or *Man Overboard*, a test of alertness.

It can be played with the children working as individuals or in teams. The Leader stands where he or she is plainly visible to all the players and performs a series of simple activities.

The children are required immediately to do exactly the opposite. If the Leader swings up the left arm the children do the same with the right, if he or she hops on the right foot, they hop on the left, and so on. Anyone making a mistake or taking too long to start the proper movement is eliminated, the last remaining person, or the last team with anyone remaining in it, being the winner.

If the children are pretty bright and alert the movements can become more complicated, *eg* one arm up, the other sideways, patting the head with one hand and rubbing the stomach with a circular motion with the other, etc.

A time limit can also be imposed, particularly if a team competition is being run, the team with the most players remaining at the end of a given time being the winner. This will help to prevent the demonstrator from becoming completely exhausted.

Man Overboard (6 plus to 10 plus. Indoors or Outdoors)

This team game can be played by both boys and girls, but is particularly suitable for small boys.

Equal teams of six to eight boys are formed. The boys stand in lines behind a Leader with a fair space (three or four feet) between each. The game Leader then calls out a series of about five orders which mean that certain actions have to be performed, the last person to carry out the order, or anyone doing the wrong thing, being considered to have been washed overboard and lost.

Anyone who suffers this fate drops out of the team and sits down away from the game. Some suggested orders are:

ALL HANDS ON DECK	Everyone 'runs on the spot'.
LOWER THE BOATS	Children haul on imaginary ropes.
DOWN BELOW	All sit on the floor with legs straight out in front of them.
SCRUB THE DECK	Kneel down and do a scrubbing action.
TURN THE CAPSTAN	All spin round on the spot.
DROP THE ANCHOR	Everyone sits cross-legged with arms folded.

The game continues for a previously arranged time, say five minutes, or until all the 'boats' except one have lost all their men overboard.

If the game is played on a time basis, the 'boat' with most players remaining in it is the winner.

River and Road (8 plus to 11 plus. Indoors or Outdoors)

This is a similar type of game to *Do This, Do That*. All the children stand in a line (put a piece of string along the ground in front of them). When the Leader says 'In the River' or just 'River' they step or jump forwards over the string. When he says 'On the Road' or 'Road' they step back over the string.

If he says 'In the River' when they are actually in the river and anyone moves, they are eliminated; similarly, if anyone moves when they are on the road and 'On the Road' is given, they drop out too. With older children particularly, an added note of suspense can be given by just using the words 'River' and 'Road' and prolonging the first letter, *ie* rolling the 'R' and saying 'R-r-r-r-r-r-r-river' or 'R-r-r-r-r-r-r-road' so that they do not know which word is coming until the very last moment.

Man the Fort (6 plus to 10 plus. Indoors or Outdoors)

A variation of *Man Overboard* with a military flavour instead of a naval one. Teams are arranged and a series of orders given, on which specific actions must be done. By failing to comply, or by not responding quickly enough, the defaulters and laggards are eliminated. Any variety of orders and actions can be devised; some suggestions are given below:

QUICK FIRE	Children stamp the feet.
SHELL FIRE	Everyone crouches down.
SALUTE THE GENERAL	All salute.
GENERAL SALUTE	All raise both arms above the head.
TANKS	Clap both hands loudly and slowly.
JEEPS	Hop on one foot.

It will be noted that in the above suggested orders there are two pairs which could well lead to some confusion; this is all to the good and helps in quick elimination.

The game should be played at least four or five times so that those who are eliminated early in the first game do have three or four more chances to do better.

All Change (6 plus to 11 plus. Indoors or Outdoors)

All the players except one sit in a circle, either on chairs or on the floor; the one remaining stands blindfolded in the centre of the circle. All the seated players then take the name of a well-known town or city, calling out the one they choose, such as London, Manchester, Bristol, Glasgow, Leeds, etc. (The Leader, or whoever is running the game, should make a mental or written note of these towns.)

The Leader then chooses two towns sitting opposite each other and calls out, 'The train is now going from London to Manchester' (or any other two places). Manchester and London get up and quietly change places; as they do so, the blindfolded one tries to catch one of them as they pass. If, after a few change-overs, no catch has been made, the Leader calls, 'All change', when everyone must cross to the opposite side of the circle. In the confusion that results the centre player is pretty certain to catch someone who then takes his place in the centre, whilst he becomes one of the 'towns'.

Frightened Animals (8 plus to 12 plus. Indoors)

All the players except one sit on chairs formed in a circle. The remaining player stands in the centre of the circle and begins to make up a story about the countryside. Whenever he mentions birds or flowers, everyone sits still, but the moment an animal of any kind is mentioned, everyone seated must move at least three seats away. During the changeover, the storyteller tries to get a seat. If he is successful, the one left out goes on with the story.

Ships in a Fog (8 plus to 12. Large room or lawn)

The children should be divided into teams of six or eight players. Two from each team represent a ship and its captain, one more is a lighthouse, and the remainder pretend to be rocks with the waves breaking around them.

The object of the game is for the 'ship' (which is blindfolded) to reach the 'lighthouse' in the shortest time.

Each team arranges itself in a way similar to that shown in Fig 27.

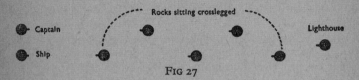

FIG 27

At the starting signal, each 'ship', with the Captain by her side, starts to move towards the 'lighthouse'—which every few seconds makes a noise to represent a foghorn or a bell. If the ship gets close to a rock the rock says 'swish, splash, swish' to represent the waves which are breaking on it.

If the 'ship' touches the 'rock' the Captain steers it twice round it and then sets the 'ship' on course again.

The first 'ship' to reach its own 'lighthouse' wins the race. Change over so that each child has a turn at being the ship, lighthouse, captain, and rocks.

Winking (11 plus to 15 plus. Indoors)

This is an age-old favourite with young boys and girls. A circle of chairs is made facing inwards. A girl sits on each chair except one, which is left empty. Behind each chair, including the empty one, stands a boy with his hands resting on top of the chair but not touching the girl sitting in it.

The boy standing behind the empty chair starts the game by winking at one of the girls, who must immediately try to leave her chair and dash to the empty one. The boy standing behind her, however, must try to stop her from going by putting his

98

hands on her shoulders. If he does this quickly enough she must remain where she is and wait for another chance when she is winked at again. If she does succeed in getting away, the boy who failed to keep her must then wink at some other girl in an effort to fill the chair in front of him. Whichever boy is doing the winking must use guile and cunning to obtain surprise. For instance, his wink can be almost imperceptible (except to the girl who is looking for it) or he can gaze steadily towards one part of the circle for a few seconds, then quickly turn his head and wink at a girl on the other side.

After all or most of the girls have been winked at, change over; let the boys sit down and the girls stand behind the chairs to have their turn at winking.

Blow the Cigarette (4 plus to any age. Indoors on a table)

Three or four players sit on each side of an ordinary table. Between them, in the centre of the table, is placed a cigarette. Each team then tries to blow the cigarette off the table on their opponent's side. In no circumstances must the cigarette be touched by the hands.

If desired, drinking straws can be used as an aid to more accurate blowing. If some of the guests at the party have colds, tactfully dissuade them from playing this and other blowing or close face contact games.

Feather Blow (6 plus to any age. Indoors)

This is an almost identical game to *Balloon Blow* except that a small, fluffy feather is used by each team. The game starts by the Leader of each team blowing his feather up in the air.

Blow Football (6 plus to any age)

This is a table game played between two sides or teams of equal number. A drinking straw is required for each person. In addition, a table-tennis ball and four matchboxes or small books (to make goals) are needed.

The players group themselves round the table (which should have a cloth on). They can be in any order, but it is preferable that one team should be towards one end of the table and the other team at the opposite end (*see* Fig 28). The matchboxes or books are then arranged as goals, about six inches wide.

The table-tennis ball is placed in the centre of the table, and

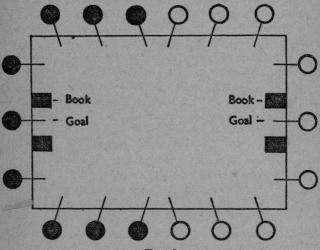

FIG 28

on the starting signal each side tries to score goals by blowing the ball into the opposing goal.

The rules are simple:

(1) There must be no pushing, shoving, or elbowing round the table.

(2) All blowing must be done through the straw.

(3) After each goal, or if the ball falls off the table, the game is restarted by placing the ball in the centre of the 'pitch'.

Fish in the Pond (6 plus to any age. Indoors or Outdoors)

Though this game needs a little previous preparation, it is well worth while, as it can cause considerable amusement without any upset—and can be used as an interlude between more strenuous activities. It can also be played by players of almost any age, boys or girls, men or women.

In essence the game is simple. All the players sit on chairs in a fairly big circle (ten to fifteen feet diameter) and fish, with rods, for the fish in the pond. The one who makes the biggest catch is the winner.

The rods are made from either pieces of dowelling or from

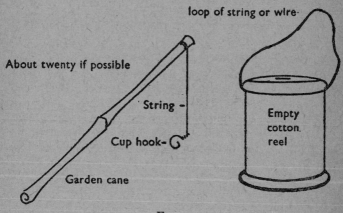

loop of string or wire

About twenty if possible

String –

Cup hook– Ᏻ

Garden cane

Empty cotton reel

FIG 29

garden canes about four feet long. The line should be a piece of string, also about four feet long, to the end of which is attached the 'hook', which can be a blunt-ended piece of wire, or better still (and less trouble) a round brass cup hook (*see* Fig 29).

The 'fish' are empty cotton reels, to the top of which is attached a loop of string or wire (Fig 29).

The 'fish' (about twenty, if possible) are placed on the ground in the centre of the circle of seated players, and on the starting signal each player does his utmost to hook as many of the 'fish' as he can.

With younger children, the winner can be decided simply on

the number of fish caught, but with older children and adults, additional interest can be raised by making each 'fish' of a different 'weight', the angler with the highest poundage taking the prize. The 'weights', *eg* 'pike, 5 lb', 'Tiddler, $\frac{1}{2}$ ounce' are written on small pieces of paper, rolling these up and slipping them into the central hole of the reel. If the reels are of various sizes it is often a good idea to put the largest 'weight' into one of the smaller reels. Fishing goes on for a given time or until all the 'fish' are caught.

Go a Different Way (6 plus to any age. Indoors or Outdoors)

This is a simple little game, but one which can cause some amusement and calls for considerable powers of invention from the players who perform late in the game.

Everyone sits round the sides of the room or lawn, leaving a space in the centre quite clear to provide a 'course' of not less than ten or twelve feet. Each player has then to go from one side of the 'course' to the other in a different way from everyone else. Here are some suggestions: walking forwards, walking backwards, walking sideways, hopping, running, hopping backwards, jumping with both feet together, with very tiny steps, with long strides, on hands and knees, on hands and toes, 'bunny'-hopping, frog-jumping, etc. If there are children of mixed ages present it is advisable to let the younger ones go early in the game and to leave the older children with the more difficult task of finding original methods of crossing the space.

Find the Leader (8 plus to 12 plus. Indoors or Outdoors)

One player goes out of the room. While he is out the others choose a Leader, and then they all sit in a circle. The Leader starts any simple movement, such as patting his stomach, opening and shutting his mouth, waving his hand, and so on. The other circle players copy his movements, changing when he does.

The player who has been outside now comes and stands in the centre of the circle. His task is to find which of the circle players is the Leader. The Leader will, of course, not normally change a movement whilst the centre player is looking in his direction. When the centre player finds the Leader, he takes his place in the circle, the Leader goes out of the room and a new Leader is chosen.

If the centre player does not discover the Leader after two or three minutes he should be told who it is; another player would then be sent out of the room and a new Leader chosen.

Dead Man (10 plus to 16 plus. Indoors or Outdoors)

Any number of players sit on the floor in a circle with their knees slightly bent and their feet together in the centre of the circle. There should be just enough room in the middle of the feet for one player to stand. All their arms are raised forwards.

The player standing in the centre holds himself absolutely rigid and then leans back on the supporting hands of the players sitting in the circle. He is then passed round the circle by each player pushing hard with his hands. Anyone who fails to pass on the 'dead man' changes places with him in the centre of the circle.

Find the Whistle (8 plus to 10 plus. Indoors or Outdoors)

This old favourite, suitable for both boys and girls, has many variations. Here is a simple form.

Two or three victims who have not played the game before go out of the room, the rest form a fairly close circle all sitting facing inwards on chairs.

The first victim is then brought in and told to kneel in the centre of the circle. He or she is then blindfolded; whilst this is being done, a small wooden whistle (one from a cracker will do), which is attached to a piece of string about twelve inches long on the end of which is a safety pin, is attached surreptitiously to the back of the victim's coat or dress.

Some rigmarole is then told about the Fairy Queen's (or Demon King's) whistle having been stolen and that it is suspected that one of the fairies (demons) in the circle has taken it. The victim has been called in to help to find it. It has got a rather unusual note, and if he (the victim) concentrates hard he may be able to hear it. At this, one of the circle players gently lifts the whistle, blows it, and lets it drop equally gently.

The blindfold is then removed. Immediately this is done, another player behind the victim blows the whistle. The victim will automatically turn round and accuse someone of having it, which will be hotly denied—and as proof, the whistle sounds again from the opposite side of the circle.

It may be quite a time before he realises that the whistle is attached to his own back.

When he does find out, allow him the privilege of 'telling the tale' to the next victim to be brought in!

Spinning the Plate (8 plus to any age)

The plate should be either a metal one or a wooden bread board. All the players sit round in a fairly wide circle, either on chairs or on the floor. They then 'number off' round the circle.

The Leader or host goes into the centre of the circle and spins the plate on the ground. He then calls out any number, and the player in the circle with that number dashes forward to catch the plate before it stops spinning. If he is successful he starts the plate spinning again and calls out another number before he returns to his place in the circle.

Anyone who fails to catch the plate either 'loses a life' or drops out. What often happens is that whilst someone is laughing at somebody else's attempts at catching the plate, his or her number is called. This fact may not be realised at all, or only at the very last instant when there is a terrific dash into the centre to catch the very last moments of the spin.

Catch the Stick (6 plus to any age. Indoors or Outdoors)

A short cane or walking stick is required. All the players except one form a fairly large circle. They then number consecutively round the circle. The remaining player stands in the centre of the circle holding the stick upright on the ground; he supports the top of it with a fingertip. Without warning, he removes his finger from the stick and calls out the number of one of the players in the circle, who must immediately dash forward and try to catch the stick before it falls to the ground. If he is unsuccessful the centre player has another turn, but if the circle player manages to catch the stick it becomes his turn to go into the centre and call out a number.

Tip It (Up Jenkins) (8 plus to any age. Indoors)

It doesn't really matter whether you call this game *Tip It* or *Up Jenkins*, it's fun either way.

Two teams, preferably of the same number of players, sit in line facing each other on opposite sides of the table.

One of the teams (chosen by tossing) passes a threepenny piece or a sixpence from hand to hand under the table. The Leader of the opposite team, after a few seconds calls out 'Up' (or 'Up Jenkins'). Immediately the team passing the coin bring their hands with fists clenched from under the table simultaneously and hold them about a foot above the table. On the second command, 'Down' or 'Down Jenkins' the clenched hands are slapped down on the table with palms flat. (Under one of them, of course, is the coin.)

The Captain or Leader of the opposite team advised by his team now has two courses open to him to find the hand covering the coin. He can either be quite definite about it, point to one of the hands and say 'Tip it' (if he is wrong the coin-holding side score a point and have another go) or he can say 'take that hand away'. If there is no coin under it, he then proceeds to order other hands to be removed from the table, one at a time. If, however, he orders a hand to be taken away and the coin *is* underneath it, the coin side wins again.

He can, if he so wishes, after having successfully moved off several hands, make another outright guess to say under which hand the coin is held. If he is successful, his side gain a point—and the coin, to try to baffle the original coin holders.

If desired, instead of the Leader giving all the orders, each member of the guessing team can give them in turn.

A further variation which can be added, and which often

causes considerable amusement, is for the guessing side, once in a game, to order 'Creepy Crawlies'. When this is given the hands which are flat on the table must be shuffled forwards about six inches by slightly raising and lowering the palm of the hand. The fingertips and the thumb are, of course, kept flat to prevent any chance of the coin being seen by the guessing side, who really hope that they may be able to hear the 'chink' on the table as the hands are moved. It rarely does!

The winning team is the one first to score a previously agreed number of points, usually an odd number such as seven, nine, or eleven.

SECTION ELEVEN
TALKING GAMES

———————————

Simple Spelling Bee (6 plus to any age)

Teams sit opposite each other in two lines. The Leader calls out a word from a pre-arranged list. The first player of one team tries to spell it. If he fails he is eliminated and the *same* word is given to the Leader of the second team. If he fails he is eliminated also. If, however, he spells the word correctly another word is given to the second player of the first team. If he in turn gets this one right, the next word is given to the second player of the second team and so on. The game ends when all the players of one team are eliminated.

In selecting words for the *Spelling Bee*, the Leader is advised not to choose difficult technical ones, but words in fairly common usage which are often spelt wrongly such as PARALLEL, JUDGMENT, BATTALION, HARASSED, EMBARRASSED, ELLIPSE, ERRATICALLY, DIPHTHERIA, HALLUCINATION, ATTACHABLE, AT-ROCIOUS, LITERARY, REHABILITATE, STATIONARY, STATIONERY, CORRESPONDENCE, and OVERREACH.

Younger players should be given simpler words or be asked to spell words which are pronounced the same as other words but spelt differently. In such cases the definition of the word should be given, *eg* PAIN, PANE; VAIN, VANE, VEIN; THERE, THEIR; WHETHER, WEATHER, WETHER; HORSE, HOARSE, etc.

Backward Spelling (8 plus to 14 plus. Indoors or Outdoors)

All the players sit in a line or circle. The Leader calls out a common word, and the first person in the line tries to spell it backwards in, say, ten seconds. If he fails he loses a 'life'. Each person in turn is given a word, and at the end of five or six rounds the one who has lost the least number of 'lives' is the winner.

The Old Oak Chest (8 plus to 12 plus)

This is an alphabetical game in which players have to think of words beginning with the letters of the alphabet in their correct order.

The players sit in a circle, and the Leader starts the game by saying, 'Up in the attic there's an old oak chest, and in that chest there's a big rosy Apple' (or some other article beginning with 'A'). The second player then says, 'Up in the attic there's an old oak chest, and in that chest there's a big white Apron' (or, like the first player, any other item he can think of beginning with 'A'). Everyone must think of something beginning with 'A' until it becomes the Leader's turn again, when he must give a word beginning with 'B'.

The game continues until all except one are eliminated, a player being eliminated, of course, if he fails to think of some item beginning with the correct letter and which has not been used by the previous players. If necessary, 'X' and 'Z' can be omitted, as there are very few words beginning with these letters.

What Are We Shouting? (10 plus to 14 plus. Indoors or Outdoors)

A noisy game, but one which can be quite amusing. Players divide into two roughly equal teams. One team then selects a proverb or saying, say, 'Too many cooks spoil the broth', and one word is allocated to each player. Thus, if there were six players, the first would be allocated 'Too', the second 'many', the third 'cooks', and so on. If there are more players than there are words in the proverb or saying, the same word is given to two or more players. For example, if there were eight in the team, the seventh player as well as the first would be allocated 'Too' and the eighth player as well as the second would be given 'many'.

All this preliminary arrangement is done quietly and out of

earshot of the opposing team. When it is done, at a signal from the Leader, the team all shout out their words at the same time, and the opposing team have to try to guess the proverb or saying. If they fail to get it on the first shout, they are allowed two more calls, and if by then they do not know what it is, the shouting team pick another proverb or saying and repeat the procedure. If, however, the listening team get the right answer, it becomes their turn to do the shouting. Whichever team gets five points first is the winner. Some suitable phrases and proverbs for this game are given below:

> Under the spreading chestnut tree.
> Jack and Jill went up the hill.
> A stitch in time saves nine.
> John Brown's body lies a-mouldering in the grave.
> Hark the Herald Angels sing.

Dumb Crambo (10 plus upwards. Indoors or Outdoors)

This noisy game, of American origin, can cause much amusement, particularly with children in their early teens.

Two teams are formed. One team, the challengers, choose an 'action' word which can be mimed readily, such as 'run', 'walk', 'hop', 'skip', 'sing', 'wave', etc. The other team are required to find this word by mime. For their guidance, the challengers' Leader gives another word which rhymes with the word required. For example, if the action word selected is 'sing', the Leader might say: 'The word we want rhymes with *king*.' The second team then seeks action words which rhyme with the word given, and mime each one in turn until they find the correct one. The challengers hoot and hiss noisily with all the incorrect mimes, but clap loudly the correct one when it is found.

In choosing action words for miming, some care should be taken to see that there are several other action words which *do* rhyme with it. Quite a number can be found for 'sing', for instance, but very few for 'walk'. The word given as a guide to the rhyme does not have to be an 'action' word.

The Queen's Kitchen (6 plus to 10 plus. Indoors or Outdoors)

Everyone sits comfortably. One player starts the game by saying, 'I am the Queen of Spain, and in the kitchen of my castle in Madrid, there is an oven of gold (or any other item which may be found in any kitchen).'

The next player repeats exactly what the first player said and adds another item. The sentence might now be: 'I am the Queen of Spain, and in the kitchen of my castle in Madrid there is an oven of gold and a silver frying pan.'

The third and subsequent players add further items, but anyone who fails to repeat *exactly* what has been said previously is eliminated or 'loses a life'.

The winner is the one who has lost the least number of 'lives' or who is the only one not to have made a mistake.

Storytellers (Teenagers and upwards)

This is a quieter game (preferably for volunteers) which can nevertheless cause considerable amusement.

The person volunteering to tell a story is given three or four objects, say a ball, a candle, a bus ticket, and a cutting from a magazine of a woman wearing a fashionable hat. He is then asked to make up a story lasting not less than two to three minutes (but not more) bringing in the objects given. When all the volunteers have told their stories, the audience vote for the one they consider to have been the most entertaining and feasible story.

Whenever possible make the objects given to the storyteller as unrelated as possible. Here are some suggestions from which you can choose:

MARBLES	CIGARETTE HOLDER	RUBBER GLOVE
BUS TICKET	SMALL TIN BOX	CLOTHES PEG
THE ACE OF SPADES	WHISTLE	BANDAGES
TINY DOLL	POTATO	DRIVING LICENCE
NEWSPAPER CUTTINGS	HAIRPIN	BISCUIT
SEASON TICKET	BABY'S NAPKIN	HOT WATER BOTTLE

BICYCLE CLIP	THREE SPENT	BLANK PIECE OF
OLD PHOTOGRAPH	MATCHES	PAPER
PAPER CLIP	DOLL'S CLOTHES	ASHTRAY, etc.
LIPSTICK	WATCH	

I Own a Garage (8 plus to 10 plus. Indoors or Outdoors)

This game is identical with *The Queen's Kitchen*, but is meant for boys. One player starts by saying, 'I am the owner of a very large garage, and in my garage I have an Austin Car.' From then onwards each player is asked to add the name of another car, anyone failing to do so, or repeating the sequence wrongly, is eliminated.

There are endless variations of this game which can be devised to suit both the age and sex of the players. Some starting sentences might be:

'I collect photographs of film stars and in my collection is a photograph of Jack Hawkins (. . . and a photograph of . . .)'.

'I am a great adventurer and on my travels I have been to San Francisco (. . . and to Timbuctoo . . .)'.

I Spy (4 plus to 7 plus. Indoors or Outdoors)

A nice quiet game for the odd moment before or after tea or between two more energetic games. The children sit about comfortably. A child is chosen to start. She says, 'I spy with my little eye something beginning with "B",' or any other letter which is the initial letter of some article *in the room*. In this case, she might be thinking of such things as button, bread, butter, basket, or book.

Each child in turn then has one guess at what the 'B' stands for. (The player must be truthful and not have in mind three or four things at the same time, finally choosing the one which no one has guessed.)

If the object is guessed correctly, the one who guesses has a turn to 'spy'.

Impossible Situations (Teenagers and upwards)

This game is similar in principle to *Storytellers*. Volunteers are asked for and are required to make up a story, the climax or part of which must be the impossible situation which is presented to them, written on a paper, two minutes before they are required to start their story. Here is an example. The first volunteer is given a piece of paper on which is written 'and there I was, at midnight, in the centre of Piccadilly wearing a tall hat, a bathing costume, and football boots'.

The storyteller must then try to make up a story to explain as reasonably as possible how he came to be in such a situation. To explain the situation by saying that the items of clothing were worn to win a bet is not permissible; every effort must be made to make the story as logical as possible so that in the end it will appear quite natural that he should find himself in such a situation.

The listeners vote for the story they consider to be the best or most ingenious explanation of the situation. Here are some more suggestions on situations:

'As I lay under the Prime Minister's dining-room table the door of the room opened and a policeman came in.'

'I realised with horror that I had just shampooed the Bishop's hair with a brilliant green dye.'

'I really had no intention whatsoever of making the Ambassador sit on a plate of ice cream.'

'And there I was standing opposite King Henry VIII in the middle of Madame Tussauds wearing a bikini.'

'And before I knew what I was doing, I was throwing jelly at the top-table guests at the Lord Mayor's banquet.'

'The President congratulated me on volunteering and shut the door of the rocket behind him.'

The Word Game (10 plus to any age. Indoors or Outdoors)

Players sit in a circle or round a table. One person thinks of a word of more than three letters and without saying what the word is calls out the first letter. Let us suppose he thinks of the word 'diver'; he calls out 'd'. The next player thinks perhaps not of 'diver' but 'dynamo', so he says 'y'. The third player not knowing what words the first two had in mind can only think of the word 'dyke' which starts with 'dy' so he says 'k'. This puts the fourth player in an impossible position, *for the object is to avoid completing a word.* All he can say is 'e' and he loses one 'life'. The fifth player would then start a new word by giving the initial letter. When any player has lost three 'lives' he is eliminated. The game continues until all except one are 'dead'; he is the winner. Certain other simple rules are advisable: (1) Proper names should not be permitted. (2) If a player has any doubts about the word in mind of the preceding player he can challenge him to give his word. If he has a legitimate word in mind, the challenger loses a 'life'; on the other hand, if the one challenged has given a wrong letter or hasn't even thought of a word but is trying to bluff, it is he, and not the challenger who loses a 'life'. An example of this is given below. The words thought of by each player are given in brackets.

First Player says 'd' (dance)
Second Player says 'i' (dimple)
Third Player says 'n' (dinner)
Fourth Player says 'o' (dinosaur)

Fifth Player cannot for the life of him think of any word starting 'dino'. He keeps a straight face and without hesitation says 'm'.

Sixth Player completely baffled by 'dinom' wonders if dynamometer is spelled with an 'i', decides it isn't, and challenges the fifth player, 'What is your word?' Player No 5 admits he hasn't been able to think of one, and thus loses a 'life'. The sixth player would then give the first letter of a new word.

SECTION TWELVE

WRITING AND QUIET GAMES

Consequence Drawing (6 plus to 10 plus. Indoors)

Pencils and paper required. This is a silly little drawing game for younger children. Each child starts off by drawing a face and neck, which can be a serious one or a funny one as desired. It is essential, however, that the drawing must be

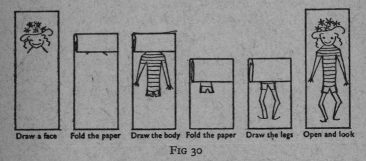

Draw a face   Fold the paper   Draw the body   Fold the paper   Draw the legs   Open and look

FIG 30

done as secretly as possible, and certainly so that the next child cannot see it. When this is done, the top of the paper is folded over so that only the bottom of the neck is visible (*see* Fig 30). The paper is then passed to the next child, who draws a body and arms. The paper is again folded and passed to a third child, who adds on the legs and feet.

The papers are then opened out, and to children the results are more often than not most hilarious.

Blindfold Drawing (6 plus to any age. Indoors)

A sheet of paper and a pencil for each competitor. The players sit round a table, or have something firm on which to rest their papers. Each player is then blindfolded. The Leader then asks them to draw something relatively simple, such as a house or a tree. When they have all finished this and almost certainly think the competition is over, the Leader asks for some additions to be made, *eg* 'Put a bird on the tree and a hill in the background' or 'Put some curtains on the windows of the house and a motor car standing in front of the garage'. If they were originally asked to draw a face, they might well be asked to put a collar and tie on the figure, or a pipe in its mouth, and so on.

The winner of the competition can be either the person who has produced the best drawing or the one whose effort is considered to be the most amusing.

Teeth Drawing (10 plus to any age)

Pencils and paper are required. This is not painful as the title suggests. Competitors are merely required to write a simple sentence, such as the first line of a nursery rhyme, or to draw a simple face, putting in the ears, eyes, nose, and mouth, but the pencil must be between the teeth to do it. The hands can be used to steady the paper or to pick up the pencil if it drops, but for no other purpose.

Wrong-handed Drawing (6 plus to any age)

Pencil and paper are required. This is a simple but often amusing competition. The players are merely asked to make a simple drawing, say a house with trees and a garden, but they must use the hand which they do not normally use, *ie* right-handed people must use the left hand, and vice versa. Give a small prize for the best effort.

Making Words (11 plus to any age)

Pencils and paper are required. The competitors are given a reasonably long word, which they write down at the top of their sheet of paper. They are then given a specified time—about ten minutes—in which to make up as many words as they can from the letters of the given word. The letters may be used in any order and for as many words as desired, but no word made must contain less than three letters. It is not usual to allow the scoring of plural words which are formed by the simple addition of the letter 's'.

In selecting the original word it is advisable to choose one with at least two or three vowels and the same number of consonants. Suppose the word chosen was 'BALUSTRADE'. A competitor might make words such as BALE, LUSTRE, TRADE, DARE, BLUSTER, DART, RAT, BARE, BUST, ART, RUST, TALE, STARE, BAT, BAR, BUT, etc.

Some useful words for this type of competition are:

ABROGATE	AUSTRALIAN	CANDIDATE
UNDERSTAND	ABORIGINE	FUNDAMENTAL
CATHERINE	TREMENDOUS	IMPERSONATE
RUSTICATE	COMBINATION	ILLUSTRATE
EMANCIPATE	INCARNADINE	RIGMAROLE
UNCONTROLLABLE	UNDERGRADUATE	PERSUADING

Find the Animals (8 plus to 14 plus. Indoors)

Each player is given a sheet of paper and a pencil. A number of short sentences are read out, which each player writes down. (Alternatively, a number of typed copies of the sentences can be prepared beforehand and handed out.) Hidden in the sentences are the names of animals which the players are asked to find. The one who discovers the most in a given time is the winner. Some sample sentences along with the answers are given below:

I would rather be rich than poor. (RAT)
I do hope that you will be a very good girl. (BEAVER)
You must try to add the number together. (TOAD)
There were ten pigeons in the loft. (PIG)
I think I made Eric understand. (DEER)
Winston Churchill is a famous Englishman. (MOUSE)
Alec owed John three shillings. (COW)
She was very early but he came late. (CAMEL)

How many times have I told you not to slam both doors. (LAMB)

I was told that I must go at nine o'clock. (GOAT)

Find the Jewels (8 plus to 14 plus. Indoors)

This is identical with *Find the Animals*, except that precious and semi-precious stones are hidden in the sentences. Five specimen sentences are given:

I have told you that you must not rub your eyes. (RUBY)

The horse had to gallop all the way. (OPAL)

In Siam and Cambodia, Monday is the day of rest. (DIAMOND)

When you go through a gate, close it after you. (AGATE)

John said, 'I must disappear like a flash.' (PEARL)

Spot the Change (6 plus to any age)

Twelve to sixteen small objects are placed neatly in three or four lines on a small tray and covered with a cloth. The players sit round the tray. The cloth is removed and the players are allowed to study the objects for one minute. They then either close their eyes or turn their backs to the tray, and whilst this is being done one object is changed over with another or into a different position and the cloth placed over the tray again. The players then open their eyes or turn round to face the tray. When they are all ready, the cloth is lifted. The first person to notice and call out what change has been made scores a point. The procedure is repeated several times, and a small prize is given to the player who either scores three or five points first, or who obtains the highest score. As an alternative to calling out, players can be given paper and pencils and asked to write down the changes made, the answers being called out after ten trials.

Consequences (10 plus to 14 plus)

Pencils and paper required. This is an old favourite, but one which never fails to amuse younger children.

The Leader of the game says, 'Write down the name of a girl.' Each child does so, folds over the top of the paper, and passes it to the next person on the right. The Leader then says, 'This girl met a boy. Write down his name.' This is done, the papers are then folded again and passed on. 'Write where they met' is the next order. Again the papers are folded over and passed on. A further series of orders are given such as, 'Write what the girl was wearing'; 'Write what the boy was wearing'; 'Write what she did'; 'Write what he did'; 'Write what she said'; 'Write what he said'; 'Write what were the consequences'.

Each child is encouraged to write humorous answers to the questions or orders. At the end the papers are unfolded and the answers, or stories, are read out. Most of them are just complete nonsense, of course—but they are often highly amusing to the guests. The sort of result that is obtained is as below:

'Mary Jones met Johnny Brown on top of a bus. She was wearing a swimming costume; he was wearing a striped suit and football boots. She cried out in terror, he laughed like mad. She said, "Will you take me to the cinema?" He said, "I think Bolton will win the cup", and the consequences were that they both caught shocking colds.'

Alphabetical Plants (10 plus to 14 plus)

Each player has a slip of paper and a pencil or pen.

A letter of the alphabet is chosen at random. (A good way to do this is to open a book at any page and take the first letter of the first word on the page.) Everyone then has to write down in five minutes as many names of plants as he can think of, beginning with the chosen letter. Suppose the letter were 'B'; the lists would then contain plants such as bluebell, buttercup, briar, blackberry, belladonna, blackthorn, etc.

At the end of the time allowed the lists are marked.

This can be done in two ways. A mark can be scored for every plant written down, or alternatively, points can be scored only for those plants which no others have got on their lists.

Geographical Games (10 plus to 14 plus)

Each player is provided with the inevitable piece of paper and a pencil. The paper is divided into four or more vertical columns. Down the left-hand column write under each other the following words: (1) country, (2) river, (3) mountains, (4) port, (5) lake, (6) sea, (7) town, (8) island, (9) race, (10) valley.

A letter of the alphabet is then chosen at random and the competitors have to try to find an appropriate word beginning with the chosen letter, which they write down in the second column. Suppose the letter chosen were 'A'. A list might then read: (1) Albania, (2) Avon, (3) Alps, (4) Antwerp, (5) Loch Awe, (6) Atlantic, (7) Andover, (8) Australia, (9) African, (10) Aylesbury.

At the end of, say, five minutes the lists are marked and the scores placed at the bottom of the columns. Another letter is then chosen and the words put in the second column, and so on until all the columns are completed. The player with the largest total at the end of the game is the winner.

Racing Between the Lines (10 plus to any age)

Provide each player with a pencil and a column of print from a newspaper. All the columns should be the same length. At the starting signal each player draws a continuous pencil line between the lines of print, starting at the top and finishing at the bottom. The first to finish wins.

Find the Town (10 plus to any age)

This is a simple jumbled-letter game. Each player is given a list of, say, ten or fifteen places with their letters all jumbled up. They are then given, say, ten minutes to try to find the actual names of the places and to write them down alongside the jumbled letters. Here are two examples. RRHWOA when re-arranged becomes HARROW, and EEARMCHNST becomes MAN-CHESTER.

Below are given twenty more examples from which a selection can be made:

FICFDRA	= CARDIFF	IBRINGHMAM	= BIRMINGHAM
LOOBNT	= BOLTON	BUHGENRID	= EDINBURGH
VREDO	= DOVER	RILECSLA	= CARLISLE
GNLEAI	= EALING	TSEBAFL	= BELFAST
FFHESEIDL	= SHEFFIELD	ONLNLDDUA	= LLANDUDNO
AHGSNITS	= HASTINGS	LLPOOERVI	= LIVERPOOL
CNROWIH	= NORWICH	NNLLCOI	= LINCOLN
RTCLSEEEI	= LEICESTER	UEANNDDLRS	= SUNDERLAND
MEAOTTTNH	= TOTTENHAM	SHREATDOL	= ALDERSHOT
GNOTHIBR	= BRIGHTON	DTBAEULNS	= DUNSTABLE

The player who gets the most right in the given time is the winner.

Sentences (10 plus to any age. Indoors)

All the competitors are asked to write the longest sentence they can without using words of more than four letters. With older children or adults one can reduce the number of letters to three. Here are two examples:

> Four-letter words: 'Mary and Tom went for a walk down the road and saw a shop that sold peas, dogs, cats, etc.'
> Three-letter words: 'Tom saw Jim on a big old log at ten to two and hit him on the ear.'

To make the game more difficult still (if you want it more difficult) ask the players to write a sentence, every word of which must consist of three letters, *eg* 'The sly dry old dog was mad, but Mum saw him run out and pat the fat red cow.'
And there will be many sillier sentences than that!

Find the Birds (Trees, Flowers) (8 plus to 14 plus. Indoors)

Sentences can be devised with hidden names of birds, trees, flowers, etc, as the occasion may demand. Below are given two or three examples in each of the above categories:

> I saw her on a bicycle in the town. (HERON)
> Caroline said that it was not worth rushing home (THRUSH)

The ancient pedlar kicked the water bucket over. (LARK)
He said that I could go as high as I wished. (ASH)
I am squire to a knight-at-arms. (OAK)
I will only go if I ride on horseback. (FIR)
That was the last error I ever made. (ASTER)
I pass the statue of Eros every day. (ROSE)
I put your pipe on your bureau. (PEONY)
His torch is just like mine. (ORCHIS)

Crossword Clues (Teenagers and upwards. Indoors)

This is a game for crossword enthusiasts, particularly those who do the more difficult ones. The clues can be made up by yourself or modified where desirable from those provided in newspapers. Each player is given, say, ten clues to solve in a given time, the one with the most correct being the winner. The following are examples:

Was the flower very cold? (BLUEBELL)
Is the God of Love really sore? (EROS)
I think the foal was idle. (LOAF)

Photographic Memory (6 plus to any age. Indoors or Outdoors)

Pencils and paper are needed. Before the party cut out about twenty pictures or photographs of articles from newspapers or magazines, such as dresses, motor cars, vacuum cleaners, wooden sheds, boot polishes, and similar items. Paste these on to a sheet of brown paper.

Allow the children to study the sheet of pictures for three or four minutes, then remove it and ask them to write down as many of the articles as they can remember. Give a small prize to the one with the most correct.

Join Them Up (10 plus to teenagers. Indoors)

Prepare a slip of paper for each guest with two lists of three-letter words such as are shown below. (Carbon copies will save a lot of writing.) Provide them also with a piece of paper and a pencil each.

The problem is to match up words from the first column with those in the second column to form six-letter words. The first player to complete the list of twenty, or the one with the most done in, say, five minutes is the winner and should be suitably rewarded.

Column 1	*Column* 2
PAR	LET
CAR	RAY
ERR	MAN
FAT	ROW
BET	SON
IMP	ANT
HAM	HER
FUR	ART
ROT	KIN
BAR	BIT
TEA	WIT
DOT	PET
SET	PET
DON	TEN
COW	HER
NAP	BOY
BUT	KEY
TIT	POT
OUT	TEE
RAT	TON

(PARSON, CARPET, HAMLET, BARMAN, BETRAY, FURROW, DOTAGE, ERRANT, FATHER, IMPART, NAPKIN, ROTTEN, TEAPOT, TITBIT, SETTEE, OUTWIT, DONKEY, RATHER, COWBOY, BUTTON)

Your Face is familiar (10 plus to teenagers)

How many times have you had to say 'your face is familiar but I can't remember your name'? Here is a quiet game based on that phrase. A little previous preparation is needed.

Cut out from an old magazine about a dozen pictures of men and women and paste them on postcards. Now make twelve small slips of paper and on each one write a name, such as ROBERT, ROGER, JANET, JOAN, and so on.

Place the pictures on the table, and place one of the names under each one. Allow the players three or four minutes to study the pictures and names; take them all away for one minute and then *replace the pictures only* in a different order. Each player has then to try to identify the pictures by name and write them down in their present order. The one with the most right wins.

To be absolutely sure *you* know the right answer put numbers on the back of the postcards and corresponding numbers on the back of the name slips.

Stepwords (9 plus to any age. Indoors or Outdoors)

Pencils and paper are required.

This is an old but ever-popular game in which one has to change one word to another in the least number of steps, altering only one letter at a time, a new word being made with each alteration. Here is an example:

Change HEAT to COLD. HEAT, HEAD, HELD, HOLD, COLD.

The alteration here has been made in four steps.

The players are given a list of five or six words which they are required to change into the words indicated. The winner is the one who makes all the changes correctly in the least number of steps.

Below are a number of suggested examples from which you can make a selection:

Change:

BLACK to WHITE	SLOW to FAST
HARD to SOFT	GOLD to LEAD
POOR to RICH	BATH to HARP
WEST to EAST	BOOT to SOCK
PINK to ROSE	HILL to VALE
COAT to DOOR	LAMB to CALF

QUIET GAMES

Difficulties (Any age from six upwards. Indoors)

A quiet game with many variations. Basically the idea is to set out five or six tests on the lines indicated below which guests try to perform in turn, the one with the highest score at the end of the tests being the winner.

(1) See how many pennies you can build into a pile on the back of the right hand which should be held out straight in front at shoulder height. Time limit, two minutes.

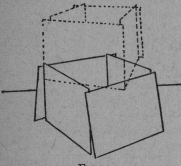

(2) Using a daily newspaper, write down the first word on the top and bottom lines of each column, starting with the front page and working through the paper. Two minutes time limit.

(3) Light as many candles as possible with a single match.

FIG 31

(4) Build the highest possible tower with playing cards you can in two minutes. If you stipulate that there should be only four cards per storey, the number of storeys can be counted (*see* Fig 31).

(5) Guess the weight of a book or other previously weighed object. Give ten points for a correct guess and deduct one point for each quarter ounce error below or above the weight.

(6) Using a straw only, transfer grains of rice from one saucer to another. The grains of rice must be kept on the end of the straw by sucking in the breath. Count one point per grain. Time limit, one minute.

(7) Using a flat ice-cream spoon (like the wooden ones supplied with tubs of ice cream) transfer as many dried peas

as possible from one small jam jar to another. Set a time limit for the task.

(8) Turn over a crown cork by stroking it with one finger as many times as possible in one minute. (One point per turn.)

(9) Judge half a minute without looking at a watch or clock. Count twenty points for a correct guess, deduct one point for each second under or over the time. (Use a stop watch for this test if possible.)

(10) Write as many words as possible starting with the letters 'AB' in one minute (*eg* about, above, abound, aboard, abdicate, ablution, etc). One point per word.

Escape (Girls 6 plus to 11 plus. Fairly large room or lawn)

The children are divided into two or more equal teams. One team are the escapers, the other the guards. The guards, blind-folded or with eyes shut, sit either on the floor or on chairs as widely spaced as possible over the room or lawn. The escapers, starting at one side of the space available, then try to tiptoe to the other side without being detected by the guards. If a guard thinks that she hears an escaper, she points; if right, the escaper is eliminated; if wrong, one member of the escaping team is allowed to reach safety.

Change over after two or three minutes and allow each team to have a turn at escaping, the team with the greatest number reaching safety being the winners of the game.

Statues (Girls 6 to 10 plus. Outdoors or Indoors)

No apparatus is needed for this game. One of the players stands close to and facing a wall, all the others behind a line or at the far end of the room or lawn.

They then begin to tiptoe towards her. The wall player can turn round as often as she wishes; if she sees anyone moving they are either eliminated or sent back to the start.

If one of the players succeeds in reaching the player at the wall and taps her, she takes her place and the game starts all over again.

SECTION THIRTEEN
HIDING AND FINDING GAMES

Hide the Thimble (4 plus to 8 plus. Indoors)

Traditionally a thimble is used for this old favourite, but any other object, such as a coin, button, or a cork can be used. One player leaves the room whilst the thimble is hidden, the remainder remain seated. The seeker comes in and begins to hunt for the thimble. Help is given by the onlookers calling out 'ice cold', 'cold', 'warmer', 'fairly warm', 'very warm', 'hot', and 'boiling' as the searcher gets nearer and nearer to the thimble.

The first searcher, when the thimble is found, then has the privilege of hiding it for the next person to find.

As an alternative to calling out 'warm', 'cold', etc, the children can hum or buzz like bees, or sing a popular song, varying the loudness or softness as the seeker approaches or recedes from the hidden object.

Find and Sit or 'Blindman' (4 plus to 10 plus. Indoors)

This is a variation of *Hide the Thimble* in which all the players are seeking at the same time. All taking part leave the room for a few moments whilst the object is placed in a not too inconspicuous spot. They then enter the room and try to find the object. The moment they see it, they do not say a word, or show by any expression that they have seen it, but sit down quietly on a chair or on the floor. The last person to discover the hidden object is the 'Blindman', but he then has the privilege of hiding it for the next round.

Find the Lot (6 plus to 12 plus. Indoors)

Pencils and paper are required. Each player is given a piece of paper on which are written the names of a number of objects which have been placed in inconspicuous but visible spots in the room. The objects must be fairly carefully chosen so that there can be no confusion with other similar or identical objects which might be normally in the room; *eg* do not write down 'A ball of wool' but 'A ball of red wool about the size of a ping-pong ball'. It is also advisable to put the chosen objects in places where they would not be in normal circumstances. The ball of wool mentioned above, for instance, might be put amongst the flowers in a vase, or a clothes peg might be resting on top of a picture or photograph.

The children then search for the objects given on the list, and whenever they find one, they write down in as few words as possible the place where it is situated. The more astute children will not stand close to one of the objects and write down the hiding place, but will almost certainly move away from it before doing any writing.

Immediately any child completes his list, he sits down. The child with the first correct list is the winner of the game. Some typical objects with suggested placings are given below for guidance:

> A brooch on top of a clock.
> A sugar lump on top of the fireplace.
> A button inside a tumbler.
> A small piece of coal on the table.
> A small mustard tin on top of a bookcase.
> A stamp wedged in the corner of a picture frame.
> A cork or bottle opener balanced on a picture rail.
> A safety pin fastened to the curtains.
> A knitting needle lying on the hearth.
> A small ball of string tied to a chair leg.

Find the Parts (8 plus to any age)

Pencils and paper are required. This is a seeking game in which all the objects are plainly visible. The game can also be used as an 'introducing game' if necessary.

Before the party, cut out from old magazines or newspapers

ten to fifteen photographs or advertisements, or even fairly large 'headlines'. Cut each one of these unevenly into two pieces and paste the whole of them quite haphazardly on three or four sheets of brown paper. Number each piece consecutively; thus if there were originally fifteen pictures, the total number of pieces would be thirty, and each one of the thirty pieces would have a number between one and thirty. Place the sheets of paper about the room, either on tables or pinned to curtains so that they are plainly visible.

Each child then goes looking at the sheets and tries to pair up the pieces, writing down side by side the two numbers which when joined together would make a complete whole.

The winner is either the player who first produces a complete and correct list, or the greatest number of correct pairings in a previously stated time.

Hidden Numbers (6 plus to 12 plus. Indoors and/or Outdoors)

Pencils and paper are required. In this seeking game the object is to find a number and write down to what the number is attached. Whilst the guests are playing a game which confines them to one room, or whilst they are having tea, arrange for a series of cards bearing consecutive numbers from 1 to 20 to be placed on or attached to various objects in the house and in the garden, if weather conditions and the time of year permit. Thus No 1 could be placed on the piano or under the piano lid, No 2 on the back of a settee, No 3 on a rose tree in the garden, No 4 on the door of the airing cupboard, and so on.

The children are given sheets of paper and pencils and told to write the numbers from 1 to 20 down the left-hand side. When they have done this they are all sent off together to find the numbers and to write down on the paper where or on what the numbers are placed.

The first child who produces a correct list, or the one who produces the most in a time of ten minutes, is judged to be the winner.

One thing must be remembered; the numbers must be so

placed that they can be seen or reached by even the smallest child in the game, otherwise the tall child will always have the advantage.

Ankle Guessing (12 plus to any age. Indoors)

This guessing game can often cause some amusement, particularly to teenagers and adults. A large screen, or something similar improvised from an old blanket or sheet, is required. The boys go out of the room whilst the girls sit behind the sheet with just their feet and ankles protruding from underneath. (The shoes should be removed.) The boys then come in and are given pencils and paper on which they write down the identities of the girls judged from the ankles on view. The girls should be numbered, say from left to right. Each boy would then put down the numbers and by the side of each a girl's name.

The one with the most correct is the winner.

The same thing can then be done the opposite way round, the girls guessing the identities of the boys. Only have volunteers for this game, someone might have a hole in his sock and not wish to display it!

Hand Guessing (12 plus to any age. Indoors)

This game is almost identical with *Ankle Guessing*, except that the girls hold one hand up above the top of the screen; the palm of the hand should be shown and not the back, as the colour of nail varnish might give away an identity. Rings and wrist watches should also be removed for the same reason.

Repeat the game with the boys behind the screen.

Bloodhounds (10 plus to any age. Indoors)

Get a number of small paper bags and punch a few tiny holes in them. Place inside each bag something which has a distinct or characteristic smell; tie up the necks of the bags and suspend them in line from a piece of string.

Each competitor, provided with a piece of paper and a pencil, then goes along the line of bags sniffing at each one and writing down what he thinks it contains. The one with the most correct wins a small prize. Suitable things to put in the bags are: mothballs, scented soap, a piece of orange-peel, some grated nutmeg, a piece of cut onion, lavender, some peppermint sweets, cinnamon, a small piece of gorgonzola, a small piece of sponge soaked in Eau de Cologne or other well-known perfume, etc.

Noises Off (8 plus to any age. Indoors)

A variation of *Pin Drop* (*see* page 142). The host goes behind a screen and produces certain noises which have to be guessed and written down by the competitors. The one with the most correct wins. Some suggested noises are: removing a crown cork from a bottle, shuffling a pack of cards, tearing a piece of paper, cracking a nut, tapping the thumbnails together, brushing a shoe or a coat, dropping a sugar lump in a cup of liquid, rubbing a bunch of keys, scratching a bottle or piece of glass with a pin, snapping a piece of wood, smoothing and folding a piece of brown paper, tapping a tumbler with a fingernail, snapping a cigarette lighter, etc.

Murder (Teenagers upwards)

This is an old game, but is ever popular with teenagers. The Leader or host prepares a number of sealed envelopes, one for each guest. All but two of the envelopes contain blank pieces of paper. One of the remaining two envelopes contains instructions such as *You are the murderer. You will strangle Mary Jones.* The second envelope merely says *You are the victim.* The envelopes are handed out at random except the one for the victim. The players open their envelopes, but do not let anyone else see whether they have received blank pieces of paper or not.

The lights are then turned out for, say, two minutes, during which time the 'murderer' gets as close to his victim as possible, having noted her position whilst the lights were still on. He then puts his hands round her neck and squeezes *very gently*. The moment the victim feels someone touching her neck she screams as loudly as possible. The 'murderer', immediately he has touched his victim, moves away from her. Ten seconds after the scream, the lights are put on again.

The Leader then chooses one of the guests to act as the detective called in to solve the murder. Everyone is instructed that they must give truthful answers to the detective's questions except the murderer, who can lie as much as he wishes.

From the answers given the detective then tries to deduce who did the murder. When he is convinced that he knows who it is, and not before, he says, 'I accuse you of murdering Mary Jones.' If his accusation is correct the murderer—for the first time, is required to tell the truth—and the detective wins. If, however, he definitely accuses the wrong person the murderer wins and the mystery remains unsolved.

Treasure Hunts (Suitable for any age above 10 plus. Indoors or Outdoors)

Treasure Hunts need some careful thought and preparation, particularly in the devising of clues, which must neither be too hard nor too easy for the age of the players taking part.

The principle of the game is simple. The players, generally in pairs, are each given a written clue to start with. The solution of the first clue leads them to the second clue, the second to the third, and so on until they finally reach the 'treasure', which can be a small prize for each of the pair. The game can be played indoors or outdoors or can go from indoor to outdoor locations, and vice versa.

As every house and every garden is different, it is obviously impossible to lay down a set of concrete instructions, but the following *Treasure Hunt* types of clues will indicate the sort of thing required for children of 12 to 14 years of age.

Each pair is given a small slip of paper on which is written:

'*Where the mouse ran up in a small bedroom*'

The smarter ones will immediately think of the nursery

rhyme 'Dickory, Dickory Dock, the mouse ran up the *clock*'. They must therefore look for a clock in a small bedroom in the house. Behind the clock is another slip of paper, written on it is: '*Motor Ad*'. This may cause a little trouble, but someone will soon see that the letters when rearranged make 'DOORMAT', and it is under the doormat that the next clue is found. This clue says, *Submarines sink under the sea. Leave out the submarines and almost go into reverse.* This when solved becomes 'Sea (see) under the sink'—so into the kitchen they go for clue 4, which reads *It's under 14 lb near a rose bush.* It will not take them long to realise that 14 lb is a *stone*, so off they go turning up stones near rose bushes—and sure enough under one of them is the fifth clue.

'*You'd be in a jam if you found the next clue on a pantry shelf.*'

This is a relatively easy one. They've got to find a jar on a shelf in the pantry.

Clues can be very simple in direction, but difficult to find. For instance, a clue could merely say *It's under a chair.* This will then involve the searchers looking under every chair in the house—and when they do find it, it is pinned underneath the seat!

The only other necessary rules are:

(1) All clues must be left where they are found.

(2) The solutions to the clues must not be given to the other treasure hunters.

(3) All cupboards, drawers, etc, must be closed if they were found so.

CHARADES AND DRAMATIC GAMES

Charades, so popular at parties in the early part of the century, are still popular with younger children (older people can play them as well) and can be introduced as 'quieteners' after a more hectic game.

The essence of the game is as follows. A word of two

or three syllables is chosen which when divided into those syllables makes two (or three) separate words. For instance, the word 'cutlass' is made up of two words 'cut' and 'lass' and the word 'wireless' of 'wire' and 'less'. Having decided upon the word, you act or mime a little sketch to illustrate each syllable in turn and then act or mime the complete word. From your three sketches (in the case of two-syllable words) the audience have to guess what the word is.

Take the word 'wireless'.

For the first syllable 'wire' you could pretend to be walking on a tightrope or pretend you were in a post office. You would then ask for a telegram form, make up a telegram (audibly) and request that it be sent off quickly.

For the second syllable 'less', if miming, you could first stretch yourself as tall as possible, then gradually make yourself smaller (less) by crouching down. If acting the syllable, you could pretend to be in a restaurant ordering a meal. You could talk to an imaginary waiter serving you with, say, potatoes. You could then say, 'No thank you, not quite so many potatoes,' indicating of course that you want 'less'.

For the complete word in mime, you could pretend to look at the *Radio Times*, select a programme, then switch on an imaginary wireless set, be a little shocked at the volume of sound, and turn it down a little.

If you are acting the word, you could visit an imaginary wireless dealer and go through a rigmarole about buying a 'set'.

If your miming or acting has been at all reasonable someone in the audience may well guess that the word you have chosen is 'wireless'.

More than one person, of course, can take part in a charade, in fact, it is better, particularly with younger children, to have at least two. In the example given two would be excellent; in the first syllable one would be the person sending the wire, the other the post-office clerk; in the second syllable one would be the diner, the other the waiter, and in the complete word, one would be the buyer of the wireless set, the other the shopkeeper. The dialogue could be quite impromptu. Below is given a short list of words suitable for miming and acting charades; the syllables are indicated:

address (add-dress)
apartment (apart-meant)
armlet (arm-let)
assent (ass-sent)
authorise (author-rise)
bedridden (bed-ridden)
behind (bee-hind)
bicycle (buy-cycle)
borax (bor-axe)
bowman (bow-man)
butterfly (butter-fly)
cargo (car-go)
carpet (car-pet)
dusty (dust-tea)
earache (ear-ache)
fellow (fell-low)
frankincense (frank-incense)
frontage (front-age)
gooseberry (goose-berry)
hammock (ham-mock)

impact (imp-act)
jargon (jar-gone)
jigsaw (jig-saw)
justice (just-ice)
kindred (kin-dread)
lapwing (lap-wing)
lipstick (lip-stick)
mandate (man-date)
marrow (mar-row)
mastiff (mast-tiff)
mischief (miss-chief)
nosegay (nose-gay)
patriot (pat-riot)
primrose (prim-rose)
rampart (ram-part)
spectacles (speck-tackles)
shocking (shock-king)
teetotal (tee-total)
undercut (under-cut)
welcome (well-come)

Miming or Acting Titles (8 plus to 12 plus. Indoors or Outdoors)

This is a variation of *Miming or Acting Nursery Rhymes*, except that songs or well-known book titles are selected by the groups. The performers can either make a little tableau, or mime or play some small scene from the book. Some suggested titles are:

Little Women	Snow White and the Seven Dwarfs
Gulliver's Travels	Ali Baba and the Forty Thieves
Robinson Crusoe	Aladdin
Dick Whittington	Johnny's so long at the fair
Robin Hood	Dashing away with a smoothing iron
Peter Pan	Underneath the spreading chestnut tree

Miming or Acting Nursery Rhymes (8 plus to 12 plus. Indoors or Outdoors)

This game is identical in character to *Miming or Acting Proverbs*, except that Nursery Rhymes form the subjects for the mimes or sketches. Here are some suggestions:

Rock-a-bye baby
Little Boy Blue
Sing a song of sixpence
Goosey-goosey Gander
Polly put the kettle on
Baa-baa black sheep
Old King Cole
Jack and Jill
Little Jack Horner
Georgie Porgie

Ding Dong Bell
Jack Sprat could eat no fat
There was a crooked man
Little Tommy Tucker
The Queen of Hearts
Baby-Baby Bunting
See Saw, Marjorie Daw
Mary had a little lamb
Mary, Mary quite contrary
Hey Diddle-Diddle

Miming or Acting Proverbs (8 plus to 12 plus. Indoors or Outdoors)

The players divide into small groups of three or four. One of the groups then goes out of the room, decides upon a proverb, and then comes back to mime or act it in front of the others, who must try to guess the proverb. Each group in turn does the same. Here are some proverbs from which a selection can be made:

Too many cooks spoil the broth.
A stitch in time saves nine.
Look before you leap.
He who hesitates is lost.
There's many a slip between the cup and the lip.
If at first you don't succeed, try, try again.
Don't put all your eggs in one basket.
A bird in the hand is worth two in a bush.
Never look a gift horse in the mouth.
It's no use shutting the door after the horse has gone.
A rolling stone gathers no moss.

People who live in glass houses shouldn't throw stones.

Take care of the pence and the pounds will take care of themselves.

Time and tide wait for no man.

Don't count your chickens before they're hatched.

Short cuts are often the longest way home.

Early to bed and early to rise make a man healthy, wealthy, and wise.

An apple a day keeps the doctor away.

It's no use crying over spilled milk.

More haste, less speed.

A nod is as good as a wink to a blind man.

Pride goes before a fall.

Nursery Rhyme Quiz (4 plus to 8 plus. Indoors)

This is another quiet 'in-between' game. All the players sit comfortably in a line or a circle. One of the grown ups then asks a series of simple questions based on Nursery Rhymes. The children are asked in turn, anyone giving the right answer scores a point. Suppose you say, 'Who was it who found the cupboard bare?' (or empty). If the first child does not know the answer you ask the second child. If he gives the right answer, you address the next question to the third child and do not start with the first again.

The questions can be worded or phrased in such a way that the game can become quite suitable for children of varying ages. Some examples are given below, the first question in each case being suitable for four- or five-year-olds, the second for, say, children of seven or eight.

(1) *a.* Whose dog didn't get a bone? ⎫
    b. Name a lady whose dog was ⎬ Mother Hubbard
       hungry ⎭

(2) *a.* Who made the girls cry when he ⎫
       kissed them? ⎬ Georgie Porgie
    b. Who didn't like playing with boys ⎭

136

(3) *a.* Who was it who lived in a shoe?
b. Who didn't know what to do about her large family? } An old woman

(4) *a.* Who had her nose pecked off by a blackbird?
b. Who was injured whilst hanging out the washing? } The maid

(5) *a.* Who wandered upstairs and downstairs?
b. Who threw an elderly gentleman down some stairs? } Goosey Gander

(6) *a.* When the sheep were in the meadow who was in the corn?
b. What animal caused damage in a cornfield? } The cow

(7) *a.* Who was a most contrary person?
b. In whose garden were a lot of pretty young ladies? } Mary(s)

(8) *a.* Who sat in a corner to eat a pie?
b. Who was it whose table manners were disgusting? } Jack Horner

(9) *a.* What was the animal that jumped over the moon?
b. Which animal flew higher than a space ship? } The cow

Any child who answers correctly scores one mark; at the end of three or four complete rounds, the child who has got the most marks gets a small prize.

With six- or seven-year-olds this can be made into a paper and pencil game. Ten or more questions are asked, then the children write down the short answers required. At the end, children change papers and mark them as the answers are called out.

Musical Sound Quiz (10 plus to any age. Indoors)

Pencils and paper are required. This quiz can be used only when a gramophone is available. Prior to the party, select about ten records. These can be a mixture of serious, light classical, or popular music according to the taste of the majority of the members of the party. Play them through and select a portion of the music which you think might be a little puzzling, part of the verse of a popular song, for example. Make a chalk mark or stick a tiny piece of paper on the record to mark the section of the record you have chosen.

Play these small selections to the contestants, who merely have to write down the name of the tune from which the music has been taken. Do not, of course, make them all difficult; put in one or two which can be recognised fairly easily, but intersperse these amongst the harder ones. If you are the fortunate possessor of a tape-recorder you can prepare a tape in advance, which will save you the trouble of having to change records during the quiz.

Tape recorders can, of course, be used to make up a variety of sound quizzes on such things as bird songs, sport's noises (an extract from a motor race, a football match, and so on), common sounds such as a dripping tap, water running out of a bath, a cork being pulled out of a bottle, a match being struck, sausages frying, or even a shovelful of coke being put on a boiler fire.

Annual Quiz (Teenagers and upwards)

Pencils and paper are required. This type of quiz is particularly suitable for Christmas or New Year's Eve parties. Devise ten or a dozen questions based on events which have happened during the year, but with each question give three suggested answers, one of which is the correct one. The players are then merely asked to write down the answer they think is right. Below are given some specimen questions of this type:

(1) The Boat Race was rowed on February 18th, May 3rd, April 5th?

(2) When did the Blankshire Conspiracy Trial take place, February, May, or July?

(3) When did the violent gale occur. The first week in January, the third week in March, or the second week in April?

(4) Did England beat the New Zealanders in the fifth Test Match by ten wickets? Two wickets? or an innings and twenty-one runs?

(5) Who won the Marathon at the Empire Games: John Brown? Herbert Black? or Augustus Green?

Even though you suggest the correct answer in each case, you will be surprised at the short memories of most of the members of your party.

Similar quizzes can be devised to suit all ages and tastes; sport, popular music, serious music, books, etc, can all form the subjects for a series of simple questions.

Topical Quiz (Teenagers and upwards)

Pencils and paper are required. Prior to the party make up a list of about ten or a dozen simple questions based on items which have been headline news during the previous three or four weeks. The answers to these questions should not require more than two or three words each.

Call out the questions, allowing half a minute or so for an answer before going on to the next. The player who has the most correct wins a small prize.

The type of question chosen can be varied to suit the ages and known tastes of the members of the party. With young people questions on sports, popular singers, dance music, etc, can be chosen; with older people, political views, trials, scandals, and so on can be introduced. Some types of questions are given below:

(1) Which team won the County Cricket Championship this year?

(2) Who won the FA Cup and what was the score?

(3) Give the names of the winners of the Men's Singles and Ladies' Singles Championship at Wimbledon.

(4) What tune was top of the Hit Parade last week?

(5) What is the name of the famous singer who was at the Palladium last week?

(6) Give the name of the film which had it's premiere a fortnight ago and who were the stars of the film?

(7) Name the person who was found guilty at the big trial at the Old Bailey this week.

(8) Who became French Premier a fortnight ago?

(9) What is the name of the prominent foreign statesman who is visiting this country at this moment?

(10) What was the headline news three days ago?

Historical Character Quiz (14 plus to any age. Indoors)

Pencils and paper are required by each player. A series of ten or twenty questions, the answer to each of which is a well-known historical character, is given. The one with the most correct wins a small prize. Here are some examples:

(1) Who was the lady whose lover expected every man to do his duty? (Lady Hamilton)

(2) He had to have his cloak washed but his action gained him favour. (Raleigh)

(3) He had a wart on his nose and he didn't like baubles. (Cromwell)

(4) She was a most distinguished fruit seller. (Nell Gwynne)

(5) By shooting arrows high in the air, his men hit more than a bull's eye. (William the Conqueror)

(6) As a widow she lived for a long time on the Isle of Wight. (Queen Victoria)

(7) His footwear is still worn a lot in winter. (Wellington)

(8) He didn't let foreigners interrupt a ball game. (Drake)

(9) A place for devotions on high ground suggests his name. (Churchill)

(10) A bird that didn't build a nest but buildings. (Wren)

Fiction Character Quiz (12 plus to any age. Indoors)

Pencil and paper are needed for each competitor. The quiz is almost identical with the one above, except that all the characters are from well-known fiction. Here are ten examples:

(1) She was Irish by name and red by colour. (Scarlet O'Hara. *Gone with the Wind*)

(2) He was a giant in one city and a dwarf in another. (Gulliver)

(3) His character was not golden but his name was quite valuable. (Long John Silver. *Treasure Island*)

(4) She was an outlaw's daughter who married a Devon man. (*Lorna Doone*)

(5) He sounds as if he plays a musical instrument. (Hornblower)

(6) Did he ever sell crazy headgear? (The Mad Hatter. *Alice in Wonderland*)

(7) His horse was black and so was his character. (Dick Turpin)

(8) An apple disagreed with her but a royal person made her well again. (Snow White)

(9) A lot of Frenchmen looked in a lot of places for him. (*The Scarlet Pimpernel*)

(10) His christian name wasn't Smith, Jones, or Brown, but it was the other even on an island. (*Robinson Crusoe*)

Tasty Dish (12 plus and upwards. Indoors)

This is yet another guessing game. Volunteers are asked for and they go out of the room. They are then led in blindfolded one at a time and are told that they are going to be given six things to taste and they have to guess what the substances are. They must be assured that there is no catch in the game, that all the things they are given are perfectly harmless and can be tasted without fear.

Previously, there should be prepared a tray containing six saucers holding a small quantity of substances such as are named below. A minute amount of each is then given to the competitor; if you can obtain a number of small, flat, wooden ice-cream spoons, so much the better, for a fresh one can be used for each volunteer.

Suitable substances are: salt, sugar, ginger, breadcrumbs, ground nutmeg, grated cheese, milk powder, cocoa, mint, small pieces of lemon rind, sherbet powder, lemonade powder, ground coconut, ground almonds, and blancmange powder.

The Pin Drop Game

All the players sit with their backs to the leader, who drops a series of common objects on to a table. The players have to guess what the object is and write its name down on the slip of paper provided. Objects such as the following are quite suitable, and not likely to damage the table surface: a pin, needle, drawing pin, thimble, small book, sponge, tennis ball, toothbrush, button, coin, paper clip, packet of cigarettes, a full and an empty box of matches, and so on.

The player who gets the most right is the winner.

SECTION FOURTEEN
SILLY GAMES

'Silly Games', that is games which are to a large extent pointless, but which nevertheless cause a considerable amount of amusement, are often useful when for no apparent reason a party is flagging a little, or in the early stages of a party before the 'ice' is properly broken. Here is a selection.

Straight Face (Any age from six upwards)

With teenagers and adults the game can be given the alternative name of *Dead Pan*.

Five or six boys are seated in a row; facing them are an equal number of girls. The girls have the task of trying to make the boys smile, the boys have to keep a 'straight face' or 'dead pan'.

At the start of the game each girl concentrates on the boy opposite to her, and by posturing, grimaces, making stupid noises, etc, she tries to make him smile. The moment any boy smiles or laughs, he drops out, and the six girls then devote their attention to the remaining five, and so on until finally there is only one boy left—he, of course, being the winner. It then becomes the task of the boys to make the girls laugh by using similar methods.

Finally, the winner from the boys and the winner from the girls try to make each other laugh. Obviously, as both have considerable control over their features, considerable ingenuity will have to be shown by each to get the other to smile—generally to the great amusement of the other guests who are watching.

Okay for Sound (6 plus to any age. Indoors or Outdoors)

A sitting-down game, useful between two energetic games. The players all sit in a circle or in a line whilst the storyteller (almost certainly yourself) makes up a story mentioning various sounds. As each one is mentioned, each child in turn has to imitate the sound to the best of his ability. Anyone failing to do so, either loses a 'life' or drops out; at the end of the story the one who has lost the least number of 'lives', or who is last in, is the winner. A typical story might start like this (the sounds to be imitated are in italics):

> 'One dark and stormy night as the wind *whistled* round the house, I heard an owl *hooting* in the trees, then somewhere a dog *barked* and a cat *mewed*. I listened for a moment. What was that? It was someone *scratching at the door*! Then there was a low *growl* and I thought I could hear someone *crying*. I got up from my chair and started to go to the door. To pretend I wasn't afraid, I started to *hum* a song, but just as I got into the hall, I heard the *scratching* and *crying* noise again, and then someone started to *cough* as well. . . .'

Other noises which could be introduced are: a train *whistled*, a motor car *started its engine*, a bell *rang*, a clock *struck three*, a *clap* of thunder, a lion *roared*, a duck *quacked*, a cock *crowed*, a horse *whinnied*, a pig *grunted*, and so on.

The story is not of vital importance with adults; in fact, the sillier it is the better, but with children it is better to try to make it reasonably interesting or dramatic.

Feed Your Friend (8 plus to any age. Indoors or Outdoors)

Two bowls, some contents for the bowls, two wooden spoons, and two aprons or overalls are required for this 'silly' game, which is a useful time-passer for the odd moments before a meal or between two hectic rushing-about games. It is also a game for volunteers only—and volunteers who do not mind looking temporarily ridiculous.

Two players, wearing overalls to protect their suits or

dresses, are seated on chairs facing each other about three or four feet apart. In their left hands they hold a small basin in which can be put some dry cereal, or broken biscuits, or if outdoors, some cereal and milk, cold rice pudding, or in extreme circumstances, some treacle. (Discretion *must* be used on the contents of the basin.) In the right hand, each player holds a wooden spoon. They are then blindfolded.

The game is quite simple. Each tries to feed the other! Don't keep them at it too long, or something somewhere will be ruined—and do make certain, particularly if liquid is involved, that their clothes are well protected.

Bun Biting (Any age from 8 upwards. Indoors or Outdoors)

This game is definitely for volunteers. Suspend one small bun (they must all be about the same size) for each competitor on a string.

Each competitor is then required to eat his bun without touching it with his hands. The one who does it first is the winner.

The Health of Colonel Bogey (14 plus to any age)

This game can be enjoyed by everyone at a party—and all can join in, young and old. A Master of Ceremonies, who has practised the whole series of movements, is the Leader.

Everyone is sitting down and has a glass with a drink (according to choice) in it. The Master of Ceremonies, who should be clearly visible to everyone, goes quite quickly through the first movements of the whole nonsense, closely watched by all the others, who are expected to do exactly as he did the moment he finishes.

The movements are these:

(1) He stands up, picks up his glass with his thumb and *one* finger, raises it shoulder high, and says, 'I drink to the health of Colonel Bogey for the first time.'

(2) He takes a short drink, sits down, and puts his glass on the table with *one* clear tap.

(3) He wipes his moustache (real or otherwise), the right side with his right hand, the left side with the left.

(4) He taps the table on the right-hand side of his glass with his right hand, and on the left-hand side with his left hand.

(5) He taps under the table, first with the right hand and then with the left.

(6) He stamps the floor, first with the right foot, then with the left, and finally—

(7) He rises a few inches from his chair and sits down again.

When all the audience have attempted to do the same the M.C. rises holding his glass with the thumb and *two* fingers and says, 'I drink to the health of Colonel Bogey for the second time.'

He then goes through the whole series of motions again, but this time he does everything *twice*, *ie* he takes two short drinks, taps twice with his glass on the table, wipes each side of his moustache twice, taps the table on each side twice, and so on, finally rising from his chair and sitting down twice.

The audience try to emulate the procedure.

The ceremony continues with everything being done *three* times (the glass being held by the thumb and three fingers) and finally *four* times, when the opening sentence is, 'I drink to the health of Colonel Bogey for the last time.'

Whatever is left in the glass must be finished off on this final toast.

Steeplechase (About 10 upwards. Indoors or Outdoors)

A short 'obstacle' course is laid out on the floor or on the lawn. The obstacles can be cushions, books, a chair laid on its side, a bucket, and so on; they should be placed about one stride apart. Two or three 'horses' are then selected and sent out of the room. The 'horses' should be players who do *not* know the game.

One of the 'horses' is then brought in to the room, shown the course, and then told that he has to walk along the course blindfolded and in no circumstances must he touch any of the obstacles.

After being given a few minutes to study the course, he is blindfolded. This should be done with a lot of chatter—and done quite slowly—but the moment the blindfold is in position, *the obstacles are very quietly removed.*

The amusement comes from watching his antics as he tries to step over the non-existent obstacles. Vocal encouragement can be given if necessary by the watchers calling out such things as 'careful, George!' or 'Ooh—you nearly touched that one!' or 'mind your left foot', and so on. When he has travelled the required distance, the 'horse' has his blindfold removed—his expression on seeing that he has been stepping over precisely nothing is also part of the fun. The obstacles are then replaced and the same procedure gone through with the remaining 'horses'.

Hat Designing (An adult game)

Give each competitor two large sheets of newspaper and half a dozen pins. Each one then tries to produce the most artistic or humorously-shaped hat possible in, say, five minutes.

Fizz-buzz (6 plus to 10 plus. Indoors or outdoors)

This is a silly little game, but useful for filling in five minutes or so between two active games or for calming down just before a meal.

All the players sit in a circle. One starts counting by saying 'One', the next says 'Two', but the third one, instead of saying 'Three', says '*Fizz*'. The fourth player says 'Four' but the fifth one says '*Buzz*'.

So the counting goes on; when a number is a multiple of three the word '*Fizz*' must be used, and when a multiple of five, the word '*Buzz*'. When a number is a multiple of both five and three, then '*Fizz-buzz*' must be called. Thus the numbers from eleven to twenty would be called: 'Eleven, *fizz*, thirteen, fourteen, *fizz-buzz*, sixteen, seventeen, *fizz*, nineteen, *buzz*'.

For the game to be effective, *the counting must be done very rapidly*. Anyone who makes a mistake either 'loses a life' or drops out.

With older children more difficulty (and amusement) can be added by using the word '*pop*' for seven and multiples of seven. The counting from eleven upwards would then become: eleven, *fizz*, thirteen, *pop*, *fizz-buzz*, sixteen, seventeen, *fizz*, nineteen, *buzz*, *fizz-pop* . . .

Sardines (Any age about 8 years upwards)

This is a variation of the universally known *Hide-and-seek*, and is particularly popular with teenagers.

The first person sent off to hide is told 'in secret' where he has to go. It might be under the stairs, under a bed, in a large cupboard or wardrobe—anywhere in fact where a number of people can crowd together if they pack themselves in very tightly. The second player (who does not know where the first one has been told to hide) then goes seeking, but is told that when he has found the first person, he does not shout out, but hides along with him. At short intervals the remaining players go seeking and are given the same instructions.

By the time half a dozen or more are packed tight like 'sardines' they will have the utmost difficulty in preventing themselves from giggling, laughing, or even screaming and thereby disclosing the hiding place.

It's pointless—but almost invariably it's fun.

Bob Apple (8 plus upwards. Indoors or Outdoors)

This is an almost identical game to *Bun Biting*, except that *peeled and cored* apples are suspended from the rope instead of buns.

Animal Feeding Time (Boys 6 plus to 10 plus. Indoors or Outdoors on a dry lawn)

This game is one that lasts only for a few minutes, but can cause considerable amusement, both for the young performers and for the onlookers.

The players sit in a fairly large circle facing inwards. In the centre of the circle is placed a bun or a bar of chocolate. You then explain that you are going to give each one the name of an animal that can be found in the Zoo, and that you will then call out the names of the animals. As soon as a player hears the name of the animal he has been given, he must dash forwards and grab the bar of chocolate; if he is not quick enough, he will be disqualified and someone else will get the opportunity.

You then go round the circle and *whisper* the name of an animal to each boy—*but you whisper the same name to all the players.* Suppose this to be 'Tiger'.

You then proceed to call out the names of animals, say, lion, giraffe, elephant, monkey, etc. As no one moves, you must pretend to look a little puzzled as if you do not understand why no one has rushed forwards. After having named half a dozen or so animals, you suddenly call out 'Tiger', and stand well clear of the seething, clawing, scrambling mass of small boys all trying to grab the same bar of chocolate at the same time.

Feeding the Baby (A silly game for adults who volunteer)

Four babies' feeding bottles, complete with teats and half full of lemonade, milk, or other drinkable liquid, are suspended (teat downwards) on pieces of string at just below head height. The competitor who succeeds in emptying his or her bottle first (it must not be touched by the hands) is the winner.

Walking the Plank (8 plus to any age. Indoors or Outdoors)

A wooden plank is required for this 'time-passer', which is similar in principle to *Steeplechase*, and should be tried only on players who have not seen it before.

The plank is placed on the floor, very slightly raised up at one end by the insertion of a couple of books underneath it. About a foot away from the raised end is placed an obstacle of some kind, such as a low stool or a chair placed on its side. Volunteers are then called for to walk the plank and jump over the obstacle. If more than one volunteers, they should be sent out of the room and called in one at a time. The first volunteer then steps on the plank and is blindfolded. He will very cautiously feel his way along the plank with his feet until he gets to the end and then prepares to jump, which he will do, and almost invariably jump quite high to make sure he gets over the obstacle. (Have someone at hand to catch him if he should stumble.)

What he does not realise, of course, is that the moment he was blindfolded, the obstacle was quietly removed, and in fact he jumped over nothing at all.

Reading in the Train (10 plus to any age. Indoors)

For this competition a number of newspapers are required; it is preferable that they should all be the same paper. Having

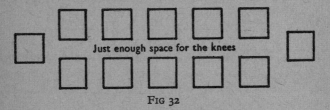

Just enough space for the knees

FIG 32

got the papers (one is required for each contestant) rearrange the page order in them. They must all be rearranged identically; inserting some upside down adds to the fun.

A circle of chairs is then made with the chairs as close together as possible, and the competitors sit on them. They are then given the disarranged newspapers and told to put all the pages in the correct order as quickly as possible. The first one to hand up his newspaper with this done is the winner. An alternative chair arrangement which makes conditions even more cramped and difficult is shown in Fig 32.

The Lift Game (10 upwards. Indoors or Outdoors)

A plank or board not less than four feet long is required for this time-passing game, which should be played only by people who have not seen it before.

Two or three volunteers are asked to 'go up in the lift' and are assured that no harm will come to them. The volunteers then leave the room and are later called in one at a time. The 'lift' is made by resting the plank on a couple of bricks or thick books about two to three inches from the ground (*see* Fig 33).

When the first volunteer is called in, he is shown the 'lift'. He is told that all he has to do is to stand on it whilst two other

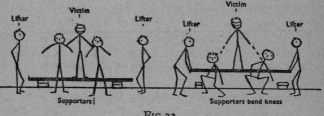

FIG 33

players try to lift him off the ground as high as they can. To make sure that he does not fall, he will be allowed to hold on to the shoulders of two other players. He then steps on to the board and is blindfolded, but is, as promised, allowed to place his hands on the shoulders of two other players standing in front of him and close to the plank (Fig 33).

Two of the stronger players in the party then grasp the ends of the plank, and with much groaning, heaving, and appropriate back-chat start to lift it slowly until it is about three inches above its supports, *ie* not more than six inches from the ground. As they begin to lift, the two players on whom the victim's hands are resting for support slowly go down into a knees-full-bend position. This will give the impression to the man on the 'lift' that he has actually risen to at least three feet or more from the ground.

At this point, the other players try to persuade him to jump down from the plank. It is almost certain that he will show considerable reluctance to do so. If he indicates that he *is* willing to do so, make certain that someone holds one or both his hands as he jumps down the six inches which he imagines to be three feet. If he refuses to jump, take off the blindfold and allow him to see exactly how far he is from the ground.

The Horror Game (Teenagers upwards)

This game can cause a considerable amount of amusement amongst teenagers and adults, but discretion must be used on whether to introduce it at a party, as the very squeamish or those with a known tendency to fainting may well find it most distasteful. Some considerable preparation is also required, as will be seen.

All the players sit round a table in complete darkness. The storyteller, being as dramatic and sepulchral as possible, tells a story of how a murder was committed and how the murderer, to hide the body, dismembered it. As each part of the body is mentioned an object is passed round under the table for each one to feel. Not until the object reaches the storyteller again does he continue his account. He might say, for instance, 'First of all the murderer chopped off the victim's head'. He then passes a cabbage or a melon round. 'Then he gouged out the eyes. . . .' (two soft grapes go round the table) 'and then the brains were removed' (a damp sponge is passed from hand to hand), and so on.

Some suitable things for various parts of the body might be as below:

> Hands. Rubber gloves stuffed with earth.
> Toes or fingers. Small, thin carrots.
> Ears. Dried figs or apricots.
> Hair. Hank of wool or silk.
> Tongue. Piece of rubber or plastic material, etc.

Chain Stores (Adults. Indoors)

This is a team game for the second half of the party, by which time everybody should be well acquainted with each other.

Two equal teams are formed; each team, if possible, should have the same number of both men and women.

The host then says that he is going shopping at one of the big chain stores in the High Street. There are (as everybody knows) two of these stores almost next door to each other, 'Cottonworths' and 'Stains & Fencer's', and what he can't buy in one, he hopes to buy in the other. He then designates one of the teams as 'Cottonworths' and the other as 'Stains & Fencer's' and goes on to explain that he is going to call out a list of articles he requires, one at a time. Each time he calls out an item, both teams (or 'stores') must try to be the first to supply him with the article called for, the one which does so scoring one point; the winning 'store' will be the one which gets the highest score.

The amusement in the game, of course, lies in the frantic rushing around to find the article demanded and to get it first to the host. Articles (which must all come from members of the team) such as the following should be demanded:

A pair of men's shoes	A key ring without any keys on it
A pair of women's shoes	Ten aspirin tablets
A collar	A diary
A tie	A cigarette case (empty)
A pair of men's suspenders	A belt
A pair of braces	Two collar studs
A lipstick	A pullover or cardigan
A powder compact	A silk scarf
An eyebrow pencil	Three twopenny stamps
Twenty cigarettes of a named brand	Two bus tickets
A handkerchief with spots on it	A luminous watch
A box of matches containing 40 matches	A bottle of scent
	A coloured pencil

The Chocolate Game (6 plus to any age. Indoors)

Three or four bars of chocolate, each one on a plate, and a number of knives and forks and a dice are required for this 'silly' game.

All the players sit crosslegged in a circle on the floor. In the centre of the circle is a bar of chocolate on a plate, by the side of which are a number of knives and forks.

Each player in turn shakes and throws the dice, but the moment anyone throws a 'six', that player dashes to the centre, picks up a knife and fork and still sitting crosslegged begins to try to eat the chocolate with the knife and fork.

In the meantime the other players are still throwing the dice. As soon as another player throws a six, the one who is busy with the chocolate dashes back to the circle and the new player, with another knife and fork continues eating what remains of the chocolate, trying to finish it before someone else throws another 'six'. Several rounds should be played, the winner of each round being the player who actually finishes each bar of chocolate.

Alternatively, the game can be made into a team competition, in which case the children would sit facing each other in two parallel lines, in the centre of which would be two plates, each containing a bar of chocolate, one for each team. Two dice would also be required, each team throwing independently of the other. In this case, the first team to finish its own bar of chocolate would be the winner.

Duck Apple (7 plus to 14)

This traditional game is more suitable for boys than for girls. Take a large bowl and fill it just above half way with water. Place the bowl on the floor (if the game is being played indoors, a waterproof groundsheet or some thick towels will prevent the carpets from getting wet.) In the bowl place one or more apples, according to the number of contestants, who should definitely be volunteers. The object of the game is quite simple, to get the apples from the water without the use of the hands.

TIME PASSERS

Don't Take the Last (8 plus upwards)

This is a game for pairs, requiring fifteen matches, which are laid out side by side on the table. Each player in turn is allowed to pick up one, two, or three matches, but no more. The object of the game is to make your partner pick up the last match. Once you know the secret and are the first player you can win every time—in this manner.

On your first pick up, take *two* matches, leaving *thirteen*. Then whatever number your opponent takes, when it is your second turn reduce the number of matches left to *nine*. (If he takes one, you take three; if he takes two, you take two; if he takes three you take one.) On the next turn, using the same method you reduce the number to *five*. Then no matter how many he takes according to rule, you can reduce the matches to *one*, which he must take on his next turn.

Missionaries and Cannibals (8 plus upwards)

This is another match problem requiring six matches, three made a little shorter than the others by snapping off the ends. The three shorter matches are the missionaries, and the three larger ones are the cannibals. The lead-up to the problem is this:

Three missionaries accompanied by three cannibals are journeying from the jungle to the coast. They come to a river which they must cross. There is a rowing boat which will carry only two people.

The problem is to get them all across the river without *at any time* there being *more* cannibals than missionaries on any side of the river. Remember that each time the boat goes from one side of the river, it must be rowed back.

Place the six matches on one side of the table, then move them across to the other side, fulfilling the above conditions.

The solution is as follows:

First Trip. A missionary and a cannibal go in the boat. The cannibal remains, and the missionary rows back.

Second Trip. Two cannibals row over, one remains, and the other rows back.

Third Trip. Two missionaries row over and a missionary and a cannibal row back.

Fourth Trip. Two missionaries row over and the cannibal already on the bank rows back.

Fifth Trip. A cannibal rows over a cannibal and rows back.

Sixth Trip. The cannibal rows over the last cannibal.

Stabbing the Thimble

This is a simple-looking little activity that is quite difficult.

Place a thimble or cork in the centre of a table.

Stand about three small paces away from the table.

Now walk quickly towards the table and on the last step close one eye, stretch out the right hand and with the index finger try to stab the thimble, and knock it over.

Five Fours are Ten

Give your friends ten coins or buttons and ask them to arrange the objects in five straight lines, each line having four coins in it. It sounds impossible at first. The solution is shown in Fig 34.

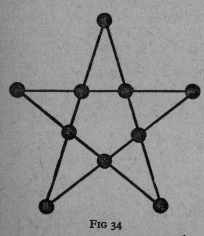

FIG 34

156

Nine Dots

Ask your guests to draw nine dots in the form of a square as shown below (Fig 35).

The problem is to draw through the nine dots with *four*

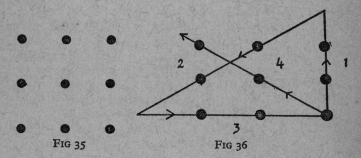

FIG 35   FIG 36

straight lines without taking the pencil off the paper and without retracing a line. Lines can cross each other if necessary.

Again, the answer is a simple one. *See* Fig 36.

The Escaping Sixpence

On a table covered with a cloth put a sixpence between two pennies; the pennies should be just the right width apart for a tumbler to rest on top of them as shown in Fig 37.

The problem is to remove the sixpence from under the tumbler *without touching the glass, the pennies, or the sixpence.*

It can be done by scratching the table cloth with the fingernail as near as possible to the glass, but without actually touching it.

Full to the Brim

Place an ordinary tumbler on a tray, then from a jug of water fill the tumbler until the water is exactly level with the top. Have available a number of pennies, about ten or a dozen will do.

Ask your guests how many pennies they think can be dropped into the tumbler without causing the water to over-

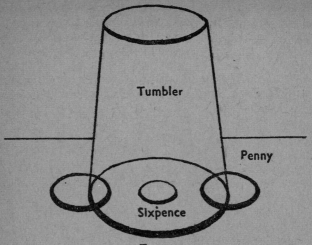

Tumbler

Penny

Sixpence

FIG 37

flow. Most of them will probably say, 'Three or four'. If, however, you slide them in edgeways, doing it very gently and not letting your fingers touch the water, you may get as many as eight or ten to go in without a drop of water spilling over.

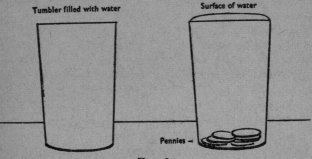

Tumbler filled with water

Surface of water

Pennies →

FIG 38

To be pretty certain of doing this, you must start off with a dry glass and above all you must ensure that when filling the tumbler, you do not wet the rim.

The reason why so many pennies can be put in, is due entirely to the surface tension of the water. If you were to look at the tumbler at eye-level you would see that the surface of the water had become shaped like a very shallow dome as shown in Fig 38.

This little trick can, if necessary, be made into a simple competition with a small prize for the one putting in the most pennies.

The Word Square Game (8 plus upwards)

Pencil and paper are required for each player. All the players draw a large square divided up into twenty-five smaller squares. (The number can be greater or less as desired.)

Each player in turn calls out a letter of the alphabet, and the players insert these letters into any of the small squares, trying to form words horizontally or vertically as they do so. The number of letters called must equal the number of squares drawn. It is also useful to stipulate that no player must call the same letter as the one immediately preceding.

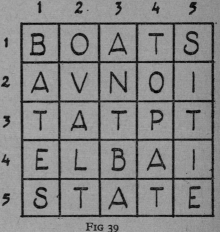

FIG 39

When the square has been filled the words which have been made are counted and one point is scored for each. One word only per row can be scored. This automatically forbids the counting of words within words or overlapping ones (*see* Fig 39).

Scoring in Fig 39 would be:

1 Across.	Either BOAT or OATS, not both	= 1 point
3 Across.	TAT only	= 1 point
4 Across.	ELBA only	= 1 point
5 Across.	STATE or ATE, not both	= 1 point
1 Down.	BATE or ATE, not both	= 1 point
2 Down.	OVAL only	= 1 point
3 Down.	ANT only	= 1 point
4 Down.	TOP or PAT, not both	= 1 point
5 Down.	SIT or TIE, not both	= 1 point
	Total	9 points

Book Cricket

This is another first-class time passer for two boys or girls on wet days either at home or at the seaside.

A book is required (or a newspaper will do) and one sheet of paper and pencil per player.

A scorer's card is made out as below:

SCORING LETTERS	PENALTY LETTERS
A = 2 runs	B = bowled out
E = 2 runs	C = caught out
I = 3 runs	L = leg before wicket
O = 4 runs	X = hit wicket
U = 6 runs	Y = run out
All other letters except penalty letters score one run.	Z = stumped

Each player then writes down the names of his team on the left-hand side of his paper, leaving space to insert the runs made by each as shown in Fig 40. The two players then toss to decide which side is to bat first.

A page of the book or newspaper is then opened and the first batsman 'goes in'. Suppose the words to be the same as at the beginning of the description of this game, and suppose May to be batting. His score will be:

1.1.3.1. 3.1. 2.1.4.1.1.2.1. 1.3.1.1.1. Caught out 29

The next batsman now 'goes in' and the scoring continues straight on. As the next letter in the sentence is 'L' poor Cowdrey is out, l.b.w. for a 'duck'.

```
┌─────────────────────────────────────────────┐
│              J. BROWN'S XI.                   │
│                                        Score  │
│  May      .    .    .    .    .    .    .      │
│  Cowdrey  .    .    .    .    .    .    .      │
│  Shepherd .    .    .    .    .    .    .      │
│  Compton  .    .    .    .    .    .    .      │
│  Bailey   .    .    .    .    .    .    .      │
│  Titmus . .    .    .    .    .    .    .      │
│  Evans    .    .    .    .    .    .    .      │
│  Wardle . .    .    .    .    .    .    .      │
│  Laker  . .    .    .    .    .    .    .      │
│  Lock     .    .    .    .    .    .    .      │
│  Trueman  .    .    .    .    .    .    .      │
└─────────────────────────────────────────────┘
```

FIG 40

When all eleven players have 'batted' another page of the book is chosen at random and the opposing side proceeds to bat. The winning side is, of course, the one that has scored the most runs. More than one innings can be played as desired.

Battleships

This is another old favourite with boys which is easier played than described—however!

Each player has a piece of paper (squared paper if you can get it) on which he draws and numbers and letters two squares each containing one hundred squares as shown in Fig 41.

Each player then draws anywhere in his own Square 'A', two battleships and two destroyers. A battleship consists of three squares with a dot (representing a gun) at each end (see Fig. 41) and destroyers of two squares each with one gun. (Notice that ships can be placed either vertically or horizontally.)

Neither player must let the other see where he has placed his ships.

A coin is tossed for the privilege of opening the firing. Let us assume that we are playing and that our opponent wins the toss and starts the battle. He is allowed six shots, one for each gun in his fleet.

He calls out a square number, say 4 A. We put a small 1 in that square. (This has been done in the diagram.) He does the same on his own Square 'B' as a record of the shots he has fired and to prevent wasting shots by firing them into the same square again.

He then calls 5 B. (This is disaster, for he has eliminated one

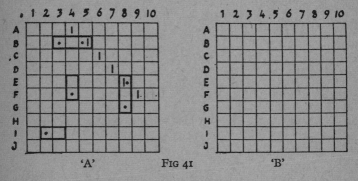

'A'   FIG 41   'B'

of our guns.) He calls 6 C. We mark it. His next shot is 7 D. His fifth shot is 8 E. (Disaster again, another gun gone!) And his last shot is 9 F.

Having fired his six shots, he is then entitled to ask, 'Have I hit anything?'

We must give a truthful answer and say, 'Yes, you have hit two battleships and knocked a gun off each.'

It is now our turn to fire, but, as two guns have been eliminated, *we have four shots only*. As we fire them, we mark them, of course, on our own Square 'B' as our record. Let us assume that we are unlucky and do not hit any of his ships.

Our opponent still has six shots, and he knows that two ships are somewhere near to his last line of shots. If he chooses to fire diagonally 5 A, 6 B, 7 C, 8 D, 9 E, and 10 F, we shall get away scot free, but if he were to fire 2 A, 3 B, 4 C, 5 D, 6 E, and 7 F, our top battleship would be completely out of action, and on our next round, we would have three shots only.

And so the game continues, each one firing in turn with the guns at his disposal, until finally all the guns of one side are out of action. The other side wins.

It is suggested that the large squares consist of 100 small squares each and that each side has only four ships, but modifications can be made at will, by having larger or smaller squares with more or less ships.

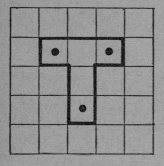 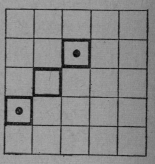

FIG 42

Variations can be added to by calling the game 'Aeroplanes' or 'Space Ships', and modifying the shape of the 'craft' put in the squares as shown in Fig 42 above. ('Space Ships' should always be placed diagonally.)

With four or more players a knockout competition can be run—and to keep everyone quiet, the losers can always play each other, or alternatively a small American type tournament can be organised in which everybody plays everybody else and the player with the most wins is the winner.

Shove-halfpenny Football (or Hockey)

This game has been popular with boys for years, and is a wonderful time passer for a wet day at home or at the seaside.

It can be played on a kitchen table, on the linoleum, or even on a very large tray. *It should not be played on the best polished table.*

Two goals, two pennies, two flat-edged combs, small rulers, set squares or protractors, and one halfpenny are required.

The goals, which should be the combined width of two pennies and a halfpenny, can be marked by matchsticks laid flat at each end of the table, by thimbles, or where possible without getting into trouble, by two pins. If none of these methods is approved, make them out of strips of cardboard as shown in Fig 43 below.

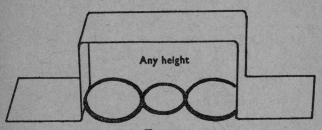

Any height

FIG 43

The object of the game is to score goals by knocking the halfpenny through the goals by means of the penny, which in turn is driven along by the flat-edged comb or ruler, each player taking it in turn to push or knock his penny (*see* Fig 44).

The game starts with a centre, one player knocking off; the opposing penny must be at least three inches away from the ball (halfpenny).

Other Rules. The game can be played for a given length of time each way (five to ten minutes) or alternatively can be decided on the best of five or seven goals.

If one player's penny strikes his opponent's penny before hitting the ball it is a foul, and the one fouled is allowed two knocks from where he was fouled. (The other penny remains where it came to rest after the foul was committed.)

If a corner is conceded, two shots are allowed from the

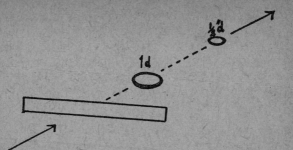

Ruler pushes penny which cannons into the halfpenny driving it forward

FIG 44

corner, *ie* the ball is knocked by the penny and then a second push is taken at the penny from where it came to rest after the first shot.

Other local rules can be devised, but the fewer there are the better.

RADIO AND TELEVISION GAMES

Many of the popular Radio and Television games can be used with advantage at a party. Where necessary they can and should be modified to suit the age of the performers. Here is a reminder selection.

Twenty Questions (Teenagers upwards)

One person, either a volunteer or chosen by lot, thinks of some person, object, or place, such as Charlie Chaplin, a frying pan, or Mount Everest. The remainder of the players then try to find out what has been chosen by asking questions, the answers to which must only be 'yes' or 'no'. If at the end of twenty questions the answer has not been discovered the questioners have lost and the same person chooses another object.

Any player who guesses the correct answer becomes the challenger.

My Wildest Dream (Teenagers upwards)

This is similar in principle to Twenty Questions except the challenger chooses his 'wildest dream'. This may include such things as 'winning the largest ever Football Pool' or 'being Prime Minister for a week'. The dreamer is questioned by the others present and must answer only 'yes' or 'no'.

Allow either a specific number of questions or fix a time limit for the questioning. If the questioners do not discover what the dream is about, the 'dreamer' has won. The questioners may make up to three direct guesses—if they fail on these the challenger again wins.

What's My Line (Teenagers upwards)

Five or six of the guests are chosen to act as challengers, the remainder become the 'panel', or if so desired, four or five only are selected to act in this capacity. Another person is chosen to act as compere to introduce the challengers.

The challengers decide what job they are supposed to do, for normally it will be little use them selecting their own, as they will probably be well known to the panel. In deciding their jobs, humorous-sounding ones can be chosen, but they must be real ones; one could have such jobs as kipper filleter, gob-stopper maker, and fluffer (a person who keeps tube railway tunnels clean), as well as the more ordinary ones such as receptionist, architect, and so on.

The 'mime' which is meant to be reasonably helpful to the panel must also be decided upon. The first challenger is then introduced and does his mime. The panel members then proceed to question him, each one continuing with his questions until he gets the answer 'no' to any one of them. The compere keeps the score of 'no's', and if the panel have not guessed the occupation before ten negative answers have been given by the challenger, he has won. Small prizes should be given to successful challengers.

Hangman (12 plus upwards. Indoors)

A slate, small blackboard, or large piece of drawing paper is required. Players divide into two teams. One team decides upon a word; one of not less than six or seven letters is preferable. Let us assume that the word chosen is 'FOOTBALL'. The leader of the challenging team then draws upon his board eight dashes to represent the letters making up the word, and at one side of the board he draws a gallows with a rope hanging from it. His board will then look like Fig 45.

The first member of the opposing side then tries to guess a letter in the chosen word. He might, for instance, say, 'Does it have an "e"?' As the word 'FOOTBALL' does not possess an 'e', no letter is put over any of the dashes, but a head is drawn on the end of the rope. The board will now appear as in Fig 46.

The next person might then say, 'Does it have an "o"?' As the word has two 'o's, these are put in over the appropriate dashes.

The game continues in this fashion. If a wrong letter is called an addition is made to the hanging body (Fig 47). For each wrong guess, of course, another part of the body is drawn until the completed man has a head, body, two arms, two legs, two eyes, a nose, and a mouth. If the side which is trying to guess the word have a total of ten wrong guesses, the man is

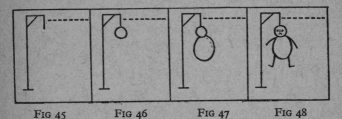

FIG 45   FIG 46   FIG 47   FIG 48

hanged and they have lost. The man will then appear as in Fig 48.

At any period of the game, a member of the guessing team, if he thinks he knows the complete word, can call it out when his turn comes. If his guess is a correct one his side wins, but if he is wrong the challenging side completes the hanging man and have another turn.

A variation of this game is to have well-known phrases or expressions such as 'HUNGRY AS A HUNTER', 'QUICK AS LIGHTNING', 'QUIET AS A MOUSE', and so on. If this variation is played, a veiled clue can be given by the challenging side. On the examples given above, for instance, the clue given for the first phrase might be 'A good shot might never be', for the second 'Certainly not a slow coach' would be appropriate, and for the third 'Hobnail boots would be useless' would be a reasonable clue.

Here are some suggested words which might be found a little puzzling to solve.

ABSCESS	BLIZZARD	CAMOMILE	DIURNAL
ABATTOIR	BRACKET	CAPILLARY	DOCILE
ABJURE	BRUSQUE	CASINO	DYNASTY
ABORIGINE	BUZZARD	CAVIARE	EASELS
ABYSMAL	CAJOLE	CHINCHILLA	ECCLESIASTIC
ACETYLENE	CALABASH	CYCLOSTILE	ELIGIBLE
ANCHOVY	CALYPSO	DISSOLUTE	FIZZLES
FRANCHISE	GALAXY	GAMMON	GHERKIN
GNOMES	GYPSIES	HOBGOBLIN	HOOPOE
HOOLIGAN	HYPERBOLA	HYSTERIA	IGLOOS
ILLICIT	INAUGURATE	INTERMIX	JUICES
KNUCKLE	LABURNUM	LATTICE	LEISURE
LENGTHY	LIEUTENANT	LIQUORICE	LLAMAS
LYMPHATIC	MAMMOTH	METAPHOR	METHYLATED
MINIMUM	MOSAIC	MYSTERY	OBNOXIOUS
OOZINESS	OMELETTE	OXYGEN	PAPOOSE
PAPYRUS	PARALYSE	PHONETIC	PHLEGM
PYTHON	QUININE	QUEUES	SANGUINE
SCIMITAR	SCISSORS	SYLLABLE	SYMMETRY
SYNAGOGUE	TYMPANY	TYPHOON	UTILITY
VOODOO	WHINNY	WRITHE	WYANDOTTE

Have a Go (Teenagers and upwards)

A good question master and one who is fairly familiar with this radio game is needed, and he should prepare beforehand a list of simple questions, from which he selects four, to ask each guest who is called out. If the guest answers all four correctly he is entitled to compete in the final or 'jack-pot' question, for which a small prize is awarded to the one giving the first correct answer.

Questions similar to, or of the type given below, are suitable ones to ask:

Who wrote *The Dancing Years*? (Ivor Novello)
Who were the four main characters in *The Three Muske-teers*? (D'Artagnan, Athos, Porthos, Aramis)

Who was the Prime Minister in 1939? (Chamberlain)

Who made the song 'Sonny Boy' famous? (Al Jolson)

Tell me the names of four Disney animals (Donald Duck, Pluto, Mickey Mouse, Dumbo, Bambi, etc)

Who went to Lilliput? (Gulliver)

How many kilometres are there in five miles? (Eight)

Who wrote *Round the World in Eighty Days*? (Verne)

Which two teams were in the 1958 Cup Final? (Bolton and Manchester United)

What is scampi? (An Italian fish like a large prawn)

What is the capital of America? (Washington)

In which country are the 'outbacks'? (Australia)

Does the camel or the dromedary have two humps? (Camel)

Give me a four-letter word ending in ENY (Deny)

In which country would you find a platypus? (Australia)

Where might you hope to find Piskeys? (Devon and Cornwall)

Where is the Land of Nod? (Yorkshire, near Hull)

Which is heavier, milk or cream? (Milk)

SECTION SEVENTEEN
MIND READING AND FORTUNE TELLING

As an interlude from rushing about or playing games which require lots of thinking and writing, an occasional demonstration of your own, or someone else's, supernatural (!) powers can often afford a few minutes relaxation for everyone. This sort of activity, however, should not be overdone, for in general most people go to a party to take part in the activities, not to watch for lengthy periods someone showing how much more clever they are than anyone else.

The following few games can be played without any elaborate preparations or memorising of difficult codes. All you need is a reliable assistant (who, if possible, should be briefed prior to the party) and a certain flair for being able to talk glibly.

X-ray Eyes

For this demonstration of your occult powers you need an opaque envelope and a small piece of paper for each guest who wishes to test your powers, which are those of being able to see what is written on a piece of paper sealed in the envelope.

Ask each person to write one or two words, or the name of some person or thing, such as 'Mother Redcap' or 'Tom Finney' or 'Cross-word Puzzle', on their pieces of paper, fold them up, and seal them in the envelopes, making absolutely certain that what they have written cannot possibly be seen through the envelope. You then collect all the envelopes.

Taking one envelope in your hand, you study it intently for some seconds, showing appropriate signs of intense concentration and making remarks such as 'Oh dear, this is a little difficult . . . wait a moment . . . yes, I think . . . I think it's something connected with a sport . . . it's . . . yes, I've got it, I think . . . I can . . . I can see a boxing-ring.' You then look hopefully and eagerly at your audience. 'I think the words are "a technical knock-out". Would anyone have written that?'

To your obvious relief and the surprise of the guest who has written it, he admits that indeed he has written these words on his piece of paper. On which admission, you casually open the envelope, glance at the paper to confirm the words, put it down on the table behind you, and take up the next envelope. Again with appropriate patter you make a correct forecast of what is written in that one—and in all the others as well.

The trick is simplicity itself.

Prior to the game you have agreed with your confederate (who takes no visible or apparent part in the game) that he will write certain words on his piece of paper, in this case, 'a technical knock-out'. When you collect the envelopes, you make absolutely certain that his envelope is put at the bottom of the pile.

When you concentrate on the top or first envelope you really haven't the faintest idea what is written inside, but when you say 'I see "a technical knock-out" ' your assistant admits that he has written such a phrase.

The audience (if they don't know the trick) will automatically assume that those words are in the envelope you are holding. When you open it and glance at the paper to make sure, you will, of course, find something completely different, say 'butter-cups and daisies'.

Thus, when you concentrate on your second envelope and make your forecast you will ultimately say. 'Yes—it's something to do with flowers—I know, "buttercups and daisies",' which some guest will immediately admit writing.

You go through all the envelopes in a similar manner. The last envelope you glance at for confirmation will contain the first phrase you mentioned, for that is the one written by your assistant.

The moment you have glanced at it, put it with the others and gather them all up promptly—*but in a haphazard manner* before the inevitable curious guest asks to have a look at them.

If you can, slip your partner's envelope under the pile, so that it appears in the nearly correct order in which you read it out.

Finding the Right Penny

This is a very simple little 'magic' game which can be played by young children from six years of age upwards.

Place about a dozen pennies in a hat or on a tray. The 'magician' then says that, blindfolded, he will pick from the pennies any one selected by the audience.

He is duly blindfolded. He then asks one of the audience to select any penny he wishes from the hat and to examine it carefully, noting the date, any peculiar distinguishing marks which may be on it, or any peculiarities of colour, so that he will have no difficulty whatsoever in recognising it again. All the other members of the audience are asked to do likewise with the penny, and when they are all quite satisfied it is dropped into the hat and all the pennies are shaken up to mix them thoroughly.

The 'magician' then gropes about amongst the coins for a moment or two and produces the correct coin, which, of course, is verified by those who examined it.

The secret? All the pennies in the hat are stone cold except one, the one that has been passed from hand to hand whilst the audience were examining it!

Naming a Chosen Object

You announce that you will go out of the room and that whilst you are out the audience must select an object in the room. On your return you will tell them what the object is.

You also say that you will require the help of your assistant, but in case anyone suspects that he is going to help you by asking questions in such a way that they form a code, every question will be worded in exactly the same way and they will be asked in a monotone—so that you cannot get any guidance from the expression in his voice. Furthermore, one or more of the audience can accompany you outside the room to make absolutely certain that you cannot, and do not, overhear what is going on inside the room.

You then go out of the room and return when called; in the meantime the audience have selected an object and have decided the way in which your assistant will ask you what it is.

You can, by the way, also stipulate that your assistant stands with his back towards you, so that you can't see his face and receive signals, such as winks or mouth movements, and that his hands are tied so that he cannot signal with them.

Your assistant then begins to question you. For example:

'Is it the clock?'
'No.'
'Is it a pack of cards?'
'No.'
'Is it a book?'
'No.'
'Is it Bill's wrist-watch?'
'No.'
'Is it the poker?'
'No.'
'Is it a wine glass?'
'Yes.'

And you are perfectly correct. The smart boy in the audience who has been watching and listening intently then pops up and says, 'I know. It was the sixth thing mentioned.'

You agree that indeed it was the sixth thing mentioned, but you are prepared to show that that is purely coincidental and has nothing to do with your power of thought reading.

Without exchanging a word with your assistant you go out again, come back and again select the right object. This time it may be the second, third, fifth, or ninth object—so that the smart boy's theory of it always being the sixth object is exploded.

The secret of the trick is again a simple one. Prior to the game you agree with your assistant on two easily remembered dates or telephone numbers, say, 6578 and 4359, or 1950 and 1870.

Taking the first two numbers as your code, the first time you come in, the sixth item mentioned is the correct one, the second time it will be the fifth item, the third time it will be the seventh, and so on.

If you select numbers or dates with an 'O' in them, this is counted as ten.

As an alternative to these four number codes, army or service numbers such as 7946278 (which are never forgotten) can be used, or even the numbers of the three or four houses adjacent to your own, such as 27, 29, 31, 33, and so on.

Naming a Card

This mind reading to select a card chosen by a member of the audience needs a fair degree of concentration both on the part of the magician and his partner. It should not be done at a party without first having had several practices. When, however, it is done well it can be quite baffling.

The trick as it appears to the onlookers is as follows:

The magician says that whilst he is out of the room anyone in the room can select any card they wish, and on his return, without touching the cards or looking at them in any way, he will, without undue trouble, name the card—which he ultimately does.

There are two steps involving the use of two simple codes to achieve the desired result.

The first thing the magician must determine is the suit in which the card is to be found.

This is determined by the position of the pack of cards on the table.

When the card has been selected by one of the audience and replaced anywhere in the pack, the pack is placed by the assistant, on the table very slightly towards one of the four sides of the table.

Thus, slightly to the north (as the magician looks at the table) indicates Clubs, slightly to the east, Diamonds, slightly to the south, Spades, and slightly to the west means Hearts (*see* Fig 49).

Even though the magician knows the suit in which the card is to be found, he does not yet declare this, but merely declares the *colour* of the suit. He then says something such as, 'I think the card is a black one, am I right?'

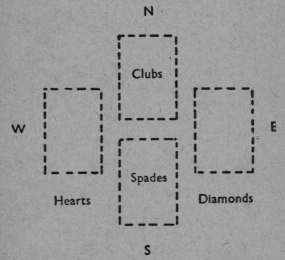

FIG 49

This is the crucial point where the second code comes in. The assistant must give one of four answers, 'Yes', 'That's right', 'You're correct', or 'Quite right'.

These answers tell the magician in which of four groups in any suit the correct card is to be found. Each suit is divided as below, the code answer to determine the group being shown alongside.

2, 3, 4, 5   in each suit = 'Yes.'
6, 7, 8, 9   in each suit = 'That's right.'
10, J, Q, K in each suit = 'You're correct.'
Ace   in each suit = 'Quite right.'

Thus, if in answer to his question as to whether the card is a black one, the assistant replied 'You're correct', the magician would know that the card is either the Ten, Jack, Queen, or King of Clubs. (He has known, of course, from the placing of the pack that the card was a Club right from the start, but hasn't yet said so.)

This he now does, for he has yet to get a code answer which will give him the exact card in the group.

He therefore says something after this fashion.

'Oh, it's a black card, I'm pretty certain it's a Club, am I correct again?'

'You're correct,' agrees his assistant.

The magician then knows that the card he is looking for is the Queen of Clubs, for 'you're correct' now indicates the third card in the group of four, thus:

    1st card in each group = 'Yes.'
    2nd card in each group = 'That's right.'
    3rd card in each group = 'You're correct.'
    4th card in each group = 'Quite right.'

If the answer 'Quite right' were given to the first query as to the colour of the suit, the magician need have no more worries at all, for 'Quite right' indicates the fourth group, which contains only the Ace. To clarify this system a little more, let us take one more example. Suppose the card selected was the Five of Diamonds.

The assistant would place the pack of cards slightly to the east of the table. The magician would then indicate, or ask if the card were a red one (he already knows it's a Diamond).

The assistant would merely reply 'Yes', indicating to the magician that it is either the Two, Three, Four, or Five of Diamonds.

The magician then says 'It is a Diamond', to which the assistant replies 'Quite right', indicating that the card is the fourth in the group.

The magician then says 'The card is the Five of Diamonds'.

The code answers can, of course, be varied slightly from

those suggested above, but they must sound quite natural and not forced or stilted.

They could be as shown below:

1st group or 1st card in each group. 'Hm. hm' or 'You're right'.

2nd group or 2nd card in each group. 'Right' or 'All right'.

3rd group or 3rd card in each group. 'O.K.' or 'Correct'.

4th group or 4th card in each group. 'You're quite right' or 'Yes'.

A different code could be used for each occasion the magician does his trick. This would almost certainly baffle even the smart onlookers, but would require a considerable amount of practice and memorising on the part of both performers.

Find the Person

The thought reader leaves the room after announcing that whilst he is outside the players must select one amongst themselves to be identified by him when he is called back.

When he is called back he looks at everyone, trying to make it appear that he is in difficulties over deciding who has been selected. Appropriate patter should also be used to add interest. After a few moments hesitation he finally points to a certain individual, who proves to be the right one.

The answer, of course, is obtained from an assistant, who in this case apparently takes no part in the game. The thought reader, however, pays particular, if somewhat surreptitious, notice of him, because he is sitting (or standing) in an identical manner as the person selected.

It may happen, of course, that the players will select the unknown assistant. This contingency must be covered by a simple code signal such as a yawn or a scratching of the ear, which will automatically mean to the thought reader that his confederate has been chosen. The fact that he yawns or scratches his ear will mean nothing to the remainder of the players, who are unaware of his part in the game.

Carrot

This is a similar thought reading game to *Find the Person* except that the assistant openly plays a part in the game.

Six objects are placed on a tray, and whilst the thought reader is out of the room one of these objects is selected by the audience inside. The assistant then calls in the mind reader, or asks someone else to call him in. When the mind reader enters, the assistant points to each of the objects in turn, after which the mind reader does a little hocus-pocus and then points to the object selected in his absence.

The code by which his assistant indicates the chosen object is given by the way he calls the mind reader back into the room and is remembered from the word CARROT.

'*C*ome in' will indicate that it is the first object which the assistant points at.

'*A*ll right' means the second object.

'*R*ight' means the third object.

'*R*eady' indicates the fourth.

'*O*.K.' signifies the fifth object.

'*T*ell him to come in.' This indicates the sixth object; the mind reader knows that the sixth has been chosen when someone other than his assistant opens the door of the room and requests him to enter.

Some members of the audience may well suspect that the code is to be found in the way the assistant calls the mind reader in, but if on occasions he asks anyone in the room to do this, their suspicions may well be allayed.

The Magic Touch

This thought reading act can be very baffling, as each time it is played the same words are used by the assistant, but a different person is involved—and what is more, the thought reader is outside the room and cannot see his assistant to obtain any visual signals.

To start, the magician (or thought reader) says that he is going out of the room; when he is out his assistant will go from person to person, putting his hands just above their heads, but when he says that he has put his hands actually on someone, he (the thought reader) will name the person concerned.

Out he goes. The assistant goes quite haphazardly from one person to another, placing both his hands above each one's head. As he does so he calls out each time, 'I raise my hands.' Finally, he calls, 'I raise my hands and place them on the head of . . .' and immediately the thought reader calls out, 'Jennifer Peniwistle', or whoever the person may be. He is right, of course.

Someone will almost inevitably say, 'Oh, you agreed that you would put your hands on Jenny on the sixth—or fifth time.' The 'magician' then says to the doubter, 'All right, when I go out of the room, *you* choose a number, and when my assistant reaches that number he will place his hands on someone's head and I will still tell you who it is.'

He goes out, and the doubter chooses any number he pleases, which he can, if necessary, whisper to the assistant. Again the assistant goes through his rigmarole, choosing players absolutely at random—and again the thought reader gives an absolutely correct answer.

The solution or code is a simple one. The assistant ultimately places his hand on the head of the person who was nearest to him on his left as the thought reader left the room. The thought reader must, of course, take particular notice of who this is, without apparently showing any interest in anyone.

The Magic Ring

This is a similar type of thought reading game to *The Magic Touch* in that no word or number code is involved.

The magician states that he will leave the room, and whilst he is out, his assistant will shake hands with someone, whom he (the magician) will identify on his return without his assistant saying a word or making any movement whatsoever.

Someone may well say, 'But you know already who it will be; you've arranged it beforehand.'

The magician, however, assures them on his honour that at this moment he has not the faintest idea who it is and, further, that from this moment he will, on his honour, not exchange a word or sign with his assistant.

The magician then goes on to explain that before this trick can be performed, a magic ring must be formed by everyone, including himself, joining hands in a circle, so that the magic power will be transmitted from everyone to himself.

Everyone then joins hands, and the magician mutters magic words and incantations. After a little of this mumbo-jumbo, he quite casually asks if anyone can feel the influence passing round the circle. He is certain to get all kinds of answers, mostly facetious. Finally, he is satisfied that the magic influence has worked and he leaves the room.

Whilst he is out, his assistant—also with some appropriate patter—shakes hands with one of those who made the magic circle.

The magician returns and after a short period of concentration, during which time he can, if he wishes, shake hands with all those who made the circle 'to see from which hand the "influence" is flowing', he decides upon a certain person, and this proves to be correct.

The method, as almost always, is simple; the assistant shakes the hand of the person who first made a remark or gave an answer when the magician asked if anyone could feel the influence passing round the circle.

Variations can be made to this code; it can be the second or third person to answer, or the first one to make a humorous remark; alternatively, it can be the third, fourth, or fifth on the left of the magician when the players formed the circle. A simple variety of codes can be used in the same game; all that is necessary is that the system shall be agreed upon and memorised by both the magician and his assistant.

Finger Plate

This is yet another simple trick involving the use of a confederate unbeknown to the rest of the players.

A coin or small object is placed on a dish or plate on the table. The thought reader then says that he will go outside the room, and whilst he is outside anyone in the room can take the object off the plate and put it into his pocket. On his return, by a very simple method he has devised, he will be able to name the person who has taken the object.

When he returns, he takes up the plate and examines it, spinning a story about polished surfaces retaining faint images of people and so on. Having spent a moment or two doing this, he then concocts some sort of a story about the final proof being obtained from fingerprints and asks the players to place their index finger on the edges of the plate, one at a time.

This they do. The magician then studies the plate intently again and finally declares that so-and-so is the culprit and has the coin. This proves to be absolutely correct.

The secret? The magician's anonymous assistant made absolutely certain that he put his finger on the plate immediately following the person who was in possession of the coin.

FORTUNE TELLING

As a quiet interlude in any party a short session of not too serious 'Fortune Telling' can be most entertaining. This is particularly so if someone at the party has done it before and has a flair for telling a story. It should be insisted, however, that the Fortune Telling is being done purely for fun and that no one must take things too seriously (despite all your warnings, someone is bound to do so) or expect things to come true.

Here is a short selection of simple fortune telling games.

Cancel Out (Any age from 8 plus upwards)

This little activity is quite useful as an 'after the meal' pastime before going on to more energetic pursuits. It can be done whilst sitting at table. Boy and girl write down their names one above the other on a slip of paper. Suppose these to be—

THOMAS WILKINSON
and
MAUREEN JOHNSON

They then cross out all the letters which are common to both names.

This leaves for the boy T W I L K I and for the girl U R E E J

These remaining letters are then counted off by calling hate, indifference, friendship, love, hate, indifference, etc. Thus the boy (working on the above plan) will be found to have indifference towards the girl, and the girl will be found to hate the boy—which will probably prove the absurdity of the game, as the two may probably be very fond of each other or even engaged!

Fortune Dice (Teenagers and upwards)

Two dice are required. The 'fortune teller' prepares a card beforehand on which is put what particular totals or combinations of numbers indicate. If possible the contents of the card should be memorised and the 'fortunes' strung together in a casual, chatty manner, or told dramatically with appropriate looks of pleasure.

The one whose fortune is to be told shakes the dice and throws them on to the table a total of seven times ('Seven is a magic number, you know').

Two things only count as far as the fortune telling is concerned, first the total score shown by the two dice at the last throw (this can be from 2 to 12) and secondly, whether there is a 'pair' or not, *ie* two threes, two fives, and so on. Here is a chart showing the significance of the throws.

(2) You may not be so lucky in the near future. Save as much as you can for a rainy day.

(3) A dark person is going to play an important part in your life in the not too distant future.

(4) You will shortly receive a letter which may be of some financial importance to you.

(5) Your kindliness and generosity may be taken advantage of by someone you know—so do be careful in what you do.

(6) A blonde person regards you with more than indifference. Look out for her (him).

(7) Your future looks quite bright. Even if you have worries now, they will soon disappear.

(8) If a red-headed person has not already entered your life, he (she) soon will and your balance is likely to be a little disturbed.

(9) Be very careful about your health—there is nothing much to worry about—but do look after yourself.

(10) You are going to get some exciting news, and someone you least expect will visit your home very soon.

(11) This means real success in what you desire most. Persevere, use tact and diplomacy and you should gain your objective.

PAIRS	SIGNIFICANCE
Two ones	A period of caution seems necessary in your affairs; step warily.
Two twos	Financial matters are going to play an important part in your life quite soon. Make the most of the situation.
Two threes	Blondes, I see nothing but blondes. They are going to mean a lot to you in one way or another.
Two fours	The sun is shining on your future—step out boldly to meet it.

PAIRS	SIGNIFICANCE
Two fives	Look after your health—keep yourself as fit as possible, as there may be a testing time not far ahead, and good health will lead to success.
Two sixes	You are indeed in luck—most of your desires will be realised—I envy you.

The fortune teller must be possessed of a quick wit and be able to gloss over apparent contradictions. Local knowledge is, of course, invaluable, and if used tactfully can lead to some humorous 'Fortunes'. The word 'tact' is perhaps the most important thing to remember. You are doing this for fun—not to upset people.

Card Fortune Telling

There are endless ways of telling 'fortunes' by cards. As with *Fortune Dice*, a fertile imagination, a little local knowledge, and an ability to explain away very glibly apparent contradictions is essential if the Fortune Teller is going to be a success.

Here is one simple method; the 'key' should be memorised if possible to add authenticity. Take a single pack of cards and discard all below the eight in each suit. Ace is high. The one who desires to know her fortune shuffles and cuts the remaining cards and hands them to the Fortune Teller, who deals them into two heaps, dealing a card to each pile in turn. The curious one is then given the opportunity of selecting one of the two piles each of which consists of fourteen cards.

The dealer then fans out face downwards the fourteen cards and asks the fortune seeker to take away four cards, leaving ten still in his hands. The four cards which have been removed are then discarded, and the ten remaining cards are laid out on the table in line, face upwards.

It is from these ten cards that the Fortune Teller has to work. A 'key' is given below.

General Indications The Fortune Teller glances at the cards and notes if there are more of one particular suit than the others, *eg* if there were five Hearts, two Clubs, one Spade, and two Diamonds, Hearts would be the dominant suit, and stress would be laid on this.

The significance of the suits are these:

HEARTS   This is the Love Suit. If this is dominant, then love matters are considered of most importance.

DIAMONDS These concern domestic and business relations.

SPADES   These concern bad luck. (Don't overstress this.)

CLUBS   The happiness or good luck cards.

Having given a general picture of the future from the whole of the ten cards, each card in turn is considered, and a meaning is attached to each. Here are some notes for guidance and from which a connected and reasonably coherent 'fortune' must be told.

HEARTS

ACE   Marriage affairs, important news, general happiness.

KING   A blond man of some importance to business or love affairs. He can be tall or short, fat or thin—and wealthy.

QUEEN A blonde woman who is destined to play an important part in the domestic life. Can be young or elderly. (Blonde can also mean 'white-haired'.)

JACK   A Don Juan (to teenagers a 'wolf') who is on the prowl. If handled correctly may be a valuable friend.

TEN   The affairs of the heart or home will flourish even though differences may temporarily upset things.

NINE   New people will be met who will bring about changes in your life. Holidays are involved.

EIGHT The affection of younger people is going to be of some importance. Patience and tolerance will lead to mutual love and trust.

DIAMONDS

ACE   Financial good fortune, a present, an important letter about money. You are going to be lucky.

KING   A ginger-haired man is due to be of some importance in your life. His influence is almost certain to be good if not at first apparent.

QUEEN The auburn-haired girl. A good business woman or home manager; she will come into your life with considerable effect.

TEN This is concerned with rings, holidays, or visits to strange places. You may be concerned in a change of occupation or home. Don't rush about, have second thoughts and then decide.

NINE You will overcome business or domestic obstacles after a struggle. Keep on persevering.

EIGHT Watch out for flatterers, particularly in your business. They may ultimately cause trouble if you do not take steps to prevent it.

SPADES

ACE You are liable to have a short spell of bad luck, but there is always a silver lining. Don't take affairs of the heart too seriously.

KING A dark man is going to mean quite a lot to you in your private or business life. His 'bark' is much worse than his 'bite'.

QUEEN The dark-haired woman of good looks and good figure will play an important part in your life after midsummer. Letters and photographs are involved.

JACK A young man of stirling worth will be of importance to your career. Don't be put off by first impressions.

TEN A change of job or residence is involved either for you or for someone you know very well indeed. Your help and advice may be needed.

NINE Do not be over-concerned with the lighter side of life. Concentrate on your present job in hand or the career you have planned.

EIGHT Music, art and literature near future. ficance to you in the near future. mean romance.

ACE   You are indeed in luck, and things are going to happen very soon. Your great desire will soon be satisfied.

KING   This dark-haired man is connected with music. If you haven't met him yet you soon will and you will fall under his good influence.

QUEEN Beware of this dark lady. She may cause considerable upset in your life. If you handle her the right way, however, the future may turn out well.

JACK   A good man, a little dull and staid at first sight, but a staunch ally on whom you can place considerable reliance.

TEN   A visit to a hospital or a doctor is possible. Do not worry unduly, things will turn out quite well. There is also some talk about an engagement which will be of interest to you.

NINE   Do not be disturbed by gossip or criticism. If you are convinced your actions are right go ahead as you have planned.

EIGHT Happiness is your ultimate destiny.

One final essential for a party Fortune Teller. Try to make all your 'clients' feel that you really know a lot more than you have disclosed—but that nevertheless you have told them quite a lot—and in fact you have confirmed what they already feel to be true.

The Wheel of Fortune (Teenagers upwards. Indoors)

This is a simple wheel game which can be constructed with little trouble before the party. Obtain a large sheet of white paper and draw on it in ink a large circle, not less than eighteen to twenty-four inches in diameter. Divide this circle up into a convenient number of segments (thirty-two is a convenient such as are given above in *Card Fortune Telling*. The circle can now be pinned to a square piece of wood or hardboard and a thin wooden or thick cardboard pointer fixed in position to make *The Wheel of Fortune* ready to use (Fig 50).

The wheel can be used on a table or on the floor with the Fortune Teller squatting crosslegged beside it in eastern fashion. (Some sun-tan make-up and a towel-turban can add to the effect.)

The one seeking to know his fortune is allowed to spin the

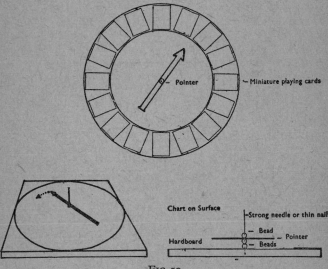

FIG 50

pointer five or seven times, and the appropriate remarks are read off the dial.

As an alternative, and to add mystery, the predictions need not be written on the wheel, but numbers only. The Fortune Teller can then have a chart or 'key' from which he can derive the answers.

A second alternative is to have playing card symbols drawn in each segment, or even to have a somewhat larger wheel, round the perimeter of which are pasted the miniature playing

189

cards which can be obtained quite cheaply from stationers or multiple stores.

A third alternative is to paint in mock Chinese or Arabic characters—each of which is given on the key with an appropriate prediction. These, however, will be more difficult to memorise.

SECTION EIGHTEEN
CARD, DICE, AND DART GAMES

In this section the more common games, such as Whist, Bridge, Nap, and Poker, are not included, as they are so well known.

Newmarket

This is a game which can be played by both children and adults and is suitable for from three to eight players. It is extremely useful as a time passer for wet days on holidays.

Two packs of cards are required, though from the second pack only four cards, an Ace, King, Queen, and Jack of different suits are required. These are the 'horses'. In addition, each player requires a supply of counters (say, twenty each), which can be beans, or peas, or matches.

The four 'horses' are placed slightly apart in the centre of the table. Each player then 'backs' a horse by placing a counter on any one of the four cards, and in addition places another counter in the centre of the table. This forms the 'kitty', which is taken by the winner.

The full pack of cards is shuffled and then dealt out with a hand to each of the players plus an additional one, *ie* if there are four players, five hands are dealt. It does not matter that some of the hands contain different numbers of cards. The dealer is permitted to look at the extra hand, and may, if he so wishes, change it for the one he has dealt to himself. If he chooses not to do this, he can 'sell it' to the highest bidder, who then takes the spare hand and discards his own.

The player immediately on the dealer's left then opens the game by placing face upwards on the table a card from any suit, providing it is the lowest of that suit he is holding. Suppose it to be the seven of diamonds. Whoever holds the eight of diamonds then places that card down on the table, face upwards in front of him. This continues until the ace is placed down, when whoever puts it down can then start a new suit by playing the lowest card of that suit that he holds. If during the playing out of a suit a player places down a card which is the same as one of the 'horses' in the centre he takes from the 'horse' any counters which may have been placed on it.

It will happen, however, that some suits are never completed, because one or more of the cards are in the extra hand which has been dealt. In such a case a 'stop' is reached and whoever played the last card must then change suits[1] and play the lowest card of any other suit he chooses from his hand.

If he does not possess cards from another suit the player on his left then has the opportunity of continuing play.

The aims of the game are two-fold, to try to get rid of a 'horse' and collect the counters from the centre card and to get rid of all the cards in your hand. The first one to do so then takes all the counters in the 'kitty', and the game starts again by players 'rebacking' a horse and placing another counter in the kitty. Any 'horses' which have not been played retain the counters on them ready for the next round.

Slap Jack (8 plus onwards)

This is an amusing game, particularly for children between the ages of eight and fourteen. It can be played by any number, but one pack of cards per four or five players is advisable. Where possible it should be played on a round table. When the cards are dealt out each player stacks them in a neat pile, face downwards in front of him but slightly to his left. Each player places his right elbow on the table with his forearm vertical; the elbow should be so placed that when the forearm is dropped the right hand will strike the centre of the table.

Starting with the player next to the dealer, each one in turn

[1] Some players insist that the *colour* of the suit must be changed, as they feel it makes a better game.

takes a card from the top of his pile and places it face upwards in the centre of the table. When a Jack appears, however, everyone in the game slaps his *right* hand down on it. The one whose hand is actually on the card (*ie* the bottom hand) takes all the cards that are in the centre and adds them to his own pile.

The player who obtains all the cards, or the most after a previously determined time, is the winner.

Old Maid

This is a card game for players of all ages, but very suitable for children. From a full pack of cards one Queen is removed. The remaining fifty-one cards are then dealt out. Some of the hands will be uneven, but this does not matter. Each player then inspects his own hand and places on the table any 'pairs' that he may have, *eg* two Sevens, two Aces, etc. If a player has three cards the same, only two of them are discarded, but if he has four, all are discarded, as they make two pairs.

When this has been done, the dealer holds out his cards (fanned out) face downwards to the next player on his left, who takes one, without, of course, knowing what it is. If it matches one in his hand he is lucky and places another pair down on the table. The third player then draws a card from the second player, the fourth from the third, and so on round and round the table. Ultimately all the cards will have been discarded in pairs, except one Queen, which cannot be made into a pair, because one Queen has been removed from the pack at the beginning of the game.

The unfortunate player holding this odd Queen becomes the 'Old Maid'.

The game is then restarted and continues for as long as desired, the winner being the one who has been the 'Old Maid' the least number of times.

Farmyards (8 plus to any age. Particularly for teenagers)

This game, ideal for four to eight people, can become really hilarious. One pack of cards per four players is advisable.

Each player is given the name of an animal with a call reasonably easy to imitate, such as a cat, dog, duck, hen, turkey, cow, horse, donkey, or sheep.

The cards are then dealt out to the players, each one stacking them in a neat pile face downwards without looking at them.

The player on the dealer's left starts the game by lifting the top card from his pile and placing it *face upwards* near to his original pile. Each player in turn does the same. When a card is turned up that 'pairs' any of the other cards showing, each of the two players concerned must immediately make the noise of the animal represented *by the other*. For example, suppose the 'cow' turns up a similar card to the one showing in front of the 'duck', the 'cow' must immediately quack and the 'duck' must moo. Whichever of the two makes the correct call first passes all his face-upwards cards to the other. This process continues until one of the players manages to get rid of all his cards. He is then the winner.

During the turning over, when any player has turned all his original pile over, he merely takes the face-upward cards, reverses them, and starts again.

Fish (Any age from 6 upwards)

This is a memory game sometimes known as '*Concentration*' or '*Pelmanism*'. It is suitable for all ages from six upwards, and can be played by two or more players.

All the cards in a pack are shuffled and then laid out fairly neatly face downwards on the table. The first player then turns face upwards any two cards. If they are a pair, *eg* two Fives or two Queens, he removes them and places them in front of him on the table. He then turns two more over. If they are not a pair he turns them face downwards again.

The other players repeat this process. After the first few players have had a turn the positions of certain cards will be known, and those who remember them are most certain to collect the greatest number of cards.

When all the cards have been picked up the player with the most is the winner.

With larger numbers, two packs of cards can be used.

Cheats (Any age from 8 upwards)

This is an amusing card game requiring no skill except perhaps the ability to keep a straight face. Suitable for four to eight players. One pack of cards is required for every four players.

The cards are dealt out and the first player to the left of the dealer who holds an Ace places it face downwards on the table, calling out 'One' as he does so. The next player then places a card face downwards, calling out 'Two'. If he does not actually hold a 'two' he still places a card down and still calls out 'Two'. The next player does the same calling out 'Three'. If, however, at any time another player thinks that someone is cheating by calling out a number and placing down a card of a different number he can challenge the player concerned by calling out 'Cheat'. The one who is accused must then turn up his card. If the accusation is true, all the players give him one of their cards; if it is false the accused gives one of his cards to the accuser. The winner of the game is the player who first gets rid of all his cards.

Authors (8 plus to any age)

This variation of *Happy Families* is suitable for four to eight players. The object of the game is to collect sets of four cards of the same value, *eg* four Aces, four Kings, four Tens, and so on.

Cards are dealt out around the players; it does not matter if the numbers turn out uneven. The player on the left of the dealer begins by asking any other player for a card of a certain denomination; he must, however, have at least one of a similar kind in his hand. If the person asked possesses such a card he hands it over. The first player can then continue to ask for the cards he needs until such time as he gets a negative reply. The player who was unable to provide the card demanded then begins to ask for the cards he wants.

The moment any player obtains four of a kind, he lays them face downwards on the table. The winner of the game is the one who finishes with the most sets of four.

Donkey

This card game is for all ages, but particularly suitable for children at a party as a relief from more hectic chasing-about games. Ideally it is played by thirteen players, as each one has four cards only. If twelve players only are available, then four cards of the same kind, *eg* four 'twos', are removed; for eleven players, all the twos and threes are taken out, and so on. The cards are dealt one at a time to the players until each has four. They then hold these in their hands ready to start. When the dealer says 'go' all the players simultaneously take a card from their hand and pass it face downwards to the next one on their left. This continues quickly and silently, each player discarding cards he doesn't require and retaining those he does *in order to obtain four of the same kind, ie* four Kings, four Queens, etc. The moment a player obtains four of a kind, he places them quietly and unobtrusively face downwards on the table and silently folds his arms. As soon as any other player sees this happen, he immediately does likewise. The last player to do this, *ie* the least observant at that moment, is the loser and becomes 'D', the first letter of Donkey. If the same player loses a second time, he becomes 'DO'. The game continues until one person has lost six times, when, of course, he will have become DONKEY. The one who has the least number of letters is the winner.

DICE GAMES

Some simple time passing games can be played with dice. If actual dice are not available, improvised ones can easily be made by spotting-in sugar lumps from one to six.

Going to Boston (6 plus upwards)

This is an American game requiring three dice which can be played by any number of players, though three or four are most suitable.

The three dice are all rolled at once. (An egg cup makes a good shaker.) The one with the largest number showing is left on the table. The two remaining dice are then shaken and rolled, and again the one with the larger number is left on the table. The third dice is then rolled and the total of the three dice is taken. That is the score of the first player.

Each player repeats this process, and the one with the highest score is the winner of the round. If two or more players have an equal number they repeat their throws until a winner is found. A given number of rounds are played, and the one who has the most wins is the winner of the whole game.

Vingt-et-un or Twenty-one (Teenagers upwards)

This is a game for any number of players, requiring one dice, and a number of matches or counters for each player.

The game starts by all the players putting one counter into the 'kitty' or pool. Each player in turn shakes and rolls the dice as many times as he wishes, trying to get a total of twenty-one or as near as possible. If he goes above twenty-one he 'busts' and is out of the game.

The player with twenty-one or the nearest to it takes all the counters in the 'kitty'. If two or more players make identical scores they can either play off or share the 'kitty'.

The important thing in the game is deciding when and when not to have another throw. If, for instance, the first four throws resulted in a 6, 3, 4, and 5, giving a total of eighteen, it would probably be better to 'stick' rather than risk another throw, for a 4, 5, or 6 would cause the player to 'bust'. If, on the other hand, the first four throws were 3, 4, 6, and 2, giving a total of fifteen, another throw at least should be taken, for if the maximum of 6 is thrown, a total of twenty-one is reached.

The game can continue for a stated number of rounds or for

a given time. The winner of the whole game is obvious; he is the one in possession of the greatest number of counters!

Round the Clock (10 plus upwards)

This is a game for three or four players, requiring two dice. Each player shakes and throws in turn, endeavouring to 'go round the clock' from one to twelve in sequence. Up to six the score on any of the dice can count, or the total showing on two of them, *eg* if a 1 and a 5 are first thrown, the player can count the 1 only. He then requires a 2. This can be obtained either by throwing a 2 and any other number, or by throwing two dice, each showing a 1. Similarly, three can be a combination of 2 and 1, four a combination of 2 and 2, or 3 and 1.

From six onwards, the score on both dice must, of course, be used. The player who first reaches twelve is the winner.

Beetle (A time passer for all ages)

This is an extremely simple game, but one which can cause a lot of fun—and even excitement—for an hour or more.

All that is required are two dice and a sheet of paper and a

Fig 51   Fig 52

pencil or pen for each player. The object of the game is to draw a beetle, like Fig 51, or, if you prefer it, a pig, like Fig 52.

If you choose a pig, call the game '*Pig*' and not '*Beetle*'.

There are certain rules which must be obeyed. In the case of *Beetle* it must be drawn in the following order: head, body,

198

legs (one at a time). In the case of *Pig*, the order is head, body, legs (one at a time) and tail.

To be entitled to draw any part, you must throw a six with the dice. Each player takes it in turn to throw both dice. If one 'six' is thrown, the head of the beetle can be drawn; if two sixes are thrown at the same time, two parts of the insect can be drawn.

In the case of *Beetle*, each player will need to throw a total of eight 'sixes' to complete his insect, one for the head, one for the body, and one for each of the six legs. (The pig needs only seven 'sixes' to complete.)

The winner of the game is the one who first completes his beetle. There are, of course, no restrictions on the species of the beetle drawn, nor on his physique, length of legs, or expression on his face!

DARTBOARD GAMES

As alternatives to the straightforward game of darts try the following little games and competitions. They can be used at a party or to provide amusement on a wet afternoon.

Short Throw Bulls-eye

Each competitor is allowed to throw three darts three times at the 'bull' from a distance of three feet. The throw must be normal in every way. The one who scores the greatest number of 'bulls' is the winner. (No! they don't all get nine!)

As a variation try doing the same thing aiming for double or treble twenty.

Ten Dart Century

This is another simple competition. Each player throws ten darts consecutively and tries to get 100 with the ten (average of ten). Darts which fall out of the board do not score but count as one of the ten.

If a dart goes outside the wire or completely misses the board, whatever number has been scored is automatically wiped out and the player is disqualified for that round.

Ten Dart Low

Ten darts are used again by each player, but the object this time is to score as few as possible with the ten. All other rules are as for *Ten Dart Century*.

Ten Dart High

A similar game to *Ten Dart Low*, except that one tries to get the highest possible score. In this game, darts which go outside the wire or off the board count as a throw but do not disqualify.

Round the Board

Each player has three darts and takes turns in throwing. The object is to throw a dart into each number moving clockwise round the board. One cannot move on until the first number is obtained. A successful throw entitles the player to attempt the next space, *eg* a player starts, aiming for the twenty; his first two darts miss, but with his third he gets it. He is now allowed to go on throwing. If he misses the 'one' with his three darts, the next player begins his throw. If he misses the 'one' with his first dart, gets it with his second, and then misses the next number with his third dart, he is not then allowed to go on but must give way to the next player. The game is won by the player who first goes all round the board and finishes with a 'bull'.

Round the Clock

The rules of this game are similar to those of *Round the Board*, except that each player starts by trying to get the 'one' first and then all the other numbers in sequence, *ie* 2, 3, 4, 5, etc, up to 20, and finally finishing with the 'bull'.

SECTION NINETEEN
GAMES FOR MOTOR-CAR JOURNEYS

Long car journeys can be boring to adults and absolute purgatory for children. When the children have exhausted their reading and drawing material, or in between times, try some of the following time passers.

Sentence Making

Each player in turn notes the first two car registration letters seen and tries to make up a sentence using the letters as the initial letters of the words, *eg* suppose the first two cars seen were 101CMP and ASQ392. A sentence has to be made with words commencing with C, M, P, A, S, and Q, such as 'Charlie meets Pat and salutes quickly'. It doesn't matter how stupid or silly the sentence is, so long as it is a sentence, *eg* with the registration letters AMX and ABV, one could say, 'A magic xylophone almost bashed Violet'.

Allow one or two minutes for a sentence to be made. If one is made in the time, one point is scored. The first player to get eleven or fifteen points is the winner.

Collecting Places

A car handbook is required and a piece of paper and a pencil for each player. Players take passing cars in turn and write down the registration letters. These are looked up in the handbook, and the name of the town or county is written alongside them.

The first player to collect ten, fifteen, or twenty different towns or counties is the winner.

Collecting Colours

Any colour (except black and white) is chosen. The players then look out for cars of the chosen colour, and immediately they see one, they call out. The first one to call out scores a point; if the calls are made simultaneously no point at all is scored. The first player to score twenty wins the game. It is better to name colours which are neither common nor rare, for in the first case a game will finish too soon, and in the second case it might never finish at all, or the children will get bored. Two colours, such as cream and blue, or cream and salmon can be used as alternatives to single colours.

Collecting Animals

Two players or more, each with a pencil and paper, are required for this game. If two are playing, one takes the near side of the road, the other the off side. If more than two are playing, divide into two teams.

The object is to spot animals which score points of the value shown below:

Ordinary cats 1 point each	Black sheep 5 points each
Black cats 5 points each	Ordinary cows 1 point each
Ordinary dogs 1 point each	Black cows 5 points each
Black dogs 5 points each	Ordinary horses 1 point each
Ordinary sheep 1 point each	Black horses 5 points each

All other animals 1 point each except monkeys 10 points, elephants 20 points, giraffes 30 points, lions 50 points, and tigers 60 points.

On ninety-nine car trips out of a hundred no one will score more than 10 points at any one time—but on the hundredth trip you *may* pass a circus!

The first player or team to score 100 points wins the game.

Collecting Cars

This game is similar to *Collecting Colours*, except that the players try to spot cars of a named make, *eg* ten Ford Consuls, ten Austins, ten Morris Minors, and so on.

Car Guessing

As a car approaches along the road, each player tries to guess its make. If two players guess the same, the one who speaks first collects a point (if the guess is correct). If they call out simultaneously no point is scored. No points are scored if the guess is made as or after the car actually passes.

Round the Clock

Players take turns in looking at car numbers on the road, *ie* the first player takes the first car that passes, the second takes the second car, and so on. The object is to collect numbers from one to twelve in the correct order. Suppose the first car that passes has a number, 3179. The first player then counts '1' because the number 3179 has a '1' in it.

The second player then has to wait for a car which passes, when it is his turn, which also has a '1' in it. The game continues until someone has got to '12'—around the clock.

A car number 1307 would not count as a '10, but 1037, or 3510 would. Similarly, 2113 would count as '11' but not 1218 because the two '1's are separated.

Score Fifty Thousand

Each player requires a pencil and a piece of paper. Again, players take cars in turn as they pass. The numbers on the registration plates are written on the papers, and the first player to reach a score of fifty thousand or more is the winner.

The number to be scored can be changed, if so desired, but should not be less than twenty thousand, as three older cars with four-figure numbers could easily end the game too soon.

Guess the Distance

An object, such as a hill, or church, or village, on the road ahead is selected, and immediately those playing try to guess the distance. This is checked from the speedometer, and the one with the nearest guess is the winner.

Blind Man's Guess

Again some object on the road ahead is selected. Players then close their eyes, and when they think the object has been reached they call 'now' and open their eyes. The one nearest the object scores a point. The player who first gets five points is the winner.

Make the Alphabet

This time passer is similar in principle to *Round the Clock*, except that instead of trying to get numbers in order, players, taking cars in turn, try to obtain the letters of the alphabet in their correct order.

More than one letter, providing they are in correct alphabetical order on the registration plate, can be scored by a player, *eg* suppose a car had registration letters AMY, then 'A' only would be scored. If the next car had BYC, 'B' only would be counted, but if the letters were BCY, then 'B' and 'C' would both be added to the 'A'.

Wild Guesses

This is a game of pure chance. When the road ahead and behind is momentarily empty, each player tries to guess either the make of the next vehicle which will appear, *eg* a Rolls Royce, a Humber, etc, or alternatively the kind of vehicle, a car, lorry, van, motor cycle, or bicycle, etc. A correct guess scores 5 points. The first player to score 50 points wins. An alternative method is to give points using the following scale for correct guesses, and to deduct, say, 1 point for incorrect guesses:

Cars, buses, trams, and lorries	2	points
Motor cycles	3	,,
Bicycles	4	,,
Motor scooters	5	,,
Tractors	6	,,
Tricycles	7	,,

Tracked vehicles	8 points
Cranes	9 ,,
Ambulances or fire engines	10 ,,

Activities for Older Children and Adults

As an occasional relief to the monotony of a long journey, older children can be given time passing tasks such as:

(1) Working out the average speed of the car at the end of each hour.

(2) Making a route mileage chart. As each place on the journey is reached, it is written down along with the number of miles from the previous place.

(3) Naming from a map each river that is crossed on certain sections of the journey.

Small sweepstakes can also be organised on such things as estimating the mileage that will be covered in the next hour, or estimating the time at which a certain town or village will be reached. In events such as these, the driver is, of course, excluded.

Licence Plate Words (Any age)

With the advent of three-letter registration marks a number of three-letter words have now been made such as EMU, FAR, POT, COW, GUM, and so on. The children take a car in turn, either approaching or passing and score one point for every word found. If desired, further interest can be added by scoring double points for animals' names.

Another alternative is to score points if the registration letters of two successive cars can be made into a word, such as JUM and PER to give JUMPER, or COW and BOY to make COWBOY. The words need not be all six-letter ones, of course, HU and MP would give HUMP or MA and NY would give MANY. Similarly, a single-letter plus a two- or three-letter registration can give a variety of words. Some examples are T and EA to give TEA, P and AT giving PAT or L and AMP for LAMP.

These games can be competitive over a short period of, say, half an hour or can be played on the length-of-the-journey basis, the words being written down in small notebooks or on postcards and the points totalled at the journey's end.

BEACH AND PICNIC GAMES

Whilst one normally associates parties with houses, many of the most successful 'get-togethers' occur during our limited summer days on the beach. Here are some suggestions for games which can be played immediately after a swim (to get warm), when the sun goes in or when that cold breeze ('you always get it about this time my dear') whistles across the beach or when the children have started to throw sand at each other and it is dropping mainly in the tea and sandwiches.

AFTER-SWIM GAMES (FOR PAIRS)

In spite of their belligerent titles these games are quite suitable for both sexes.

Knee Boxing

Skip about lightly and try to tap your partner's knees with your flat hands. He, of course, is trying to do exactly the same to you.

Chinese Boxing

Partners face each other holding up both arms. Each then grasps the other's *left wrist* with his own *right hand*. This leaves the *left hand* free. With this free hand each tries to tap the other on top of the head without having his own tapped in a similar manner.

Advantage Wrestle

All you have to do in this game is to try to get *behind* your partner, grasp him round his waist, and lift him off the ground

—making certain that he does not succeed in doing exactly the same to you.

Danish Wrestling

Opponents stand facing each other, right foot touching right foot, each grasping the other's right hand. Now, by pulling, pushing, or twisting, each one tries to make the other move his right foot from position. The left foot can be moved about quite freely. After a little while, change hands and feet—left foot to left foot, left hand grasping left hand.

Foot Fencing

Again partners stand facing each other. Moving about very lightly each one tries to touch the other's feet with his toes. The touch must be as light as possible; stamping, hacking, and kicking should *definitely* be discouraged.

Sawing Wood

Partners stand close to each other with the left leg forwards, hands clasped, one arm straight, the other bent. A sawing-like action is then done. It is advisable to start slowly and work up to a good fast rhythm with the trunk twisting round as much as possible.

Duck Fighting

Short doses of this activity are recommended, otherwise the knees will ache too much. Face your partner in the knees full bend position with the arms forward. Now by hopping about quite freely on both feet try to make your partner fall over or touch the sand with his hands. You can do this by slapping his hands with your own, or making him miss when he tries to do the same to you.

Elbow Tug-of-war (Any age)

Draw three straight lines on the sand about ten to fifteen feet apart. Partners stand on the centre line and link their right or left arms at the elbows. Each then tries to tug the other backwards to his rear line. Change elbows and repeat.

Coffee Grinding (Any age)

Partners face each other, both with arms raised midway upwards. They grasp each other's hands. Keeping their hands firmly clasped, they turn under their hands until standing back to back. They continue the turning movement until they are back to their starting position.

They then try to do this complete movement for as long as and as fast as they possibly can.

Hopping Tug-of-war (6 and upwards)

Partners face each other grasping hands and standing on one foot. They then try to tug each other backwards over a pre-arranged distance. Draw three lines as in *Elbow Tug-of-war*.

Hopping Neck Wrestle (8 and upwards)

More suitable for boys. Partners stand on one foot and clasp each other round the neck with both hands. By pulling, pushing, tugging, and twisting, each tries to make the other put his raised foot to the ground. Change feet and repeat the activity.

Lift the Jelly Fish (6 and upwards)

Partners should preferably be about the same size and weight. One lies on the dry sand completely relaxed. His partner then tries to pick him up and carry him a short distance of, say, ten yards. If the lying partner remains perfectly limp and does not assist in any way, the standing partner will find that lifting him is a most difficult operation indeed.

Lifting the Sack or Weighing Salt (8 and upwards)

Partners of about equal size and weight stand back to back and link elbows tightly. First one and then the other bends forwards and lifts his partner off the ground. The movement must be made rhythmical to get the most benefit from it.

Obstinate Calf (6 and upwards)

Partners stand facing each other. One half-crouches, half-kneels, facing the other and looking up, *ie* the head must be kept well pressed back. The standing partner clasps the kneeling one round the back of the neck with both hands then tries to pull him forwards. The 'calf' resists and tries to move backwards.

Obstinate Wheelbarrow (6 and upwards)

Partners take up a 'wheelbarrow' position. The standing partner tries to push the 'wheelbarrow' forwards; the wheelbarrow, however, is prepared to go in any direction but forwards, and avoids this by turning, twisting, and wriggling.

Bull Fight (8 and upwards)

Definitely a boy's activity. Partners face each other on hands and knees. Each then tucks his head under the other's left shoulder and tries to push his opponent backwards along the sand.

ACTIVITIES FOR THREES AND FOURS

Break-out (6 and upwards)

This is an energetic game for four or more. Three players join hands to make a circle, the fourth stands inside the circle. On the word 'Go', the centre player tries to break out of the circle, the other three doing their utmost to prevent this happening. Each player should have a turn inside the circle.

One Against Three (6 and upwards)

Four players. Three join hands to make a circle. The fourth stands outside the circle and indicates one of the circle players that he will try to touch. The circle players try to prevent this happening by spinning round. The outside player must run round the circle to try to make his touch. Each player should have a turn outside the circle.

Poison (6 and upwards)

Four or more players. A circle of about three feet diameter is drawn, or a towel is placed on the sand. The players join hands in a circle round it. Then by pulling, pushing, and tugging, each player tries to make someone else step into the circle or on to the towel without doing so himself.

King of the Ring (8 and upwards)

This game is more suitable for boys and men, though, no doubt, tomboys would more than hold their own.

A fairly large circle is drawn on the sand, inside which all the players stand. Then by pulling, pushing, dragging, heaving, and charging each player tries to get someone to step outside the ring without doing so himself. The last person to remain in the circle becomes 'King of the Ring'.

Races and Relays (Any age)

There is an almost infinite variety of races and relays that can be devised for the beach. A number of such races are given on pp. 75–93. Use these as they are, or adapt them to suit the occasion and location.

Immediately after a swim, 'all in' races are more suitable than Relays, where players wait for a turn to perform. A simple race of the 'all-in' type is:

Racing Against a Ball

Two lines are drawn about thirty to forty yards apart. The Leader and all the players stand on one of the two lines. The Leader then throws or rolls a small ball towards the other line, and all the players try to race it to the line. A fair amount of judgment is required on the part of the thrower, so that it is 'touch and go' as to whether the ball or one of the players wins the race.

Other suggestions for 'all-in' races are Hopping, Running Backwards, Running on all Fours (Monkey Race), Wheelbarrow Races (Partners), Jumping off both Feet (Kangaroos).

GAMES FOR LARGER NUMBERS

The eleven games given in this section require a minimum of marking and equipment; nothing more than a large rubber ball and spades are required for any of them. Obvious and well-known games such as football and cricket have been omitted, the stress being placed on games which are suitable for both sexes and whose rules are so extremely simple that even young children can learn them in a few minutes.

Three Passes (8 and to any age, boys or girls)

One ball, of any size, only is required; suitable for four to twelve players. Each player has a partner. The object of the game is for each pair to make three consecutive good passes between each other, *eg* Jack to Jill, Jill to Jack, Jack to Jill. Other players, of course, are trying to intercept the passes and get hold of the ball to make their own passes. The passes are made from hand to hand, but with boys only, foot passing can be substituted if desired.

The Leader starts the game by throwing up the ball, and after any pair have made three passes the game stops for a moment. The Leader restarts the game by again throwing up the ball. The first pair to make three passes five times are the winners.

In order to prevent the players scattering all over the beach, it is advisable to draw a rectangle on the sand about twenty yards long by ten yards wide and confine the game to that area.

Spade Ball (8 and to any age)

This team game is for sides of five to eleven players, more if needs be, requiring one ball (a large rubber one if possible), and two spades or sticks.

A simple court about twenty yards by ten yards is marked out as shown in Fig 53. Two circles, one at each end, are drawn; these should be about six feet in diameter. In the centre of each circle is stuck the spade or stick.

Note. If there are only five-a-side, the size of the court can be reduced to, say, fifteen yards by eight yards.

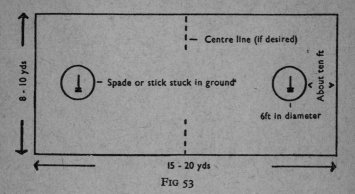

FIG 53

The object of the game is for each side to hit or knock down with the ball, the spade or stick in their opponents' circle.

Rules

(1) The game is started by the referee throwing up the ball between two players from opposing sides, standing in the centre of the court.

(2) All passes must be made by hand.

(3) There must be no running with the ball (as in Rugby). It must be passed immediately it is received.

(4) There is no kicking, tackling, pushing, or charging allowed. Rough play of any kind is forbidden.

(5) In each circle a goalkeeper stands. He is not allowed to leave this circle.

(6) No one except the goalkeeper is allowed to enter the circles.

(7) If a goalkeeper knocks down his own spade it counts as one point to the opposing side. All other goals, *ie* hits on the spade, count as two points.

(8) The game is played for an equal length of time each way.

(9) Play can take place behind as well as in front of the circles.

(10) Throw-ins, corners, etc, are as in Football or Hockey.

Any other rules can be made, if desired, but the fewer there are consistent with the safety of the players, the easier and more enjoyable will be the game for everyone.

Philadelphia Kick Ball (10 and upwards)

This is a form of rounders (of American origin) only requiring one ball of any size from a tennis ball to a football and a simple court marking as shown in Fig 54.

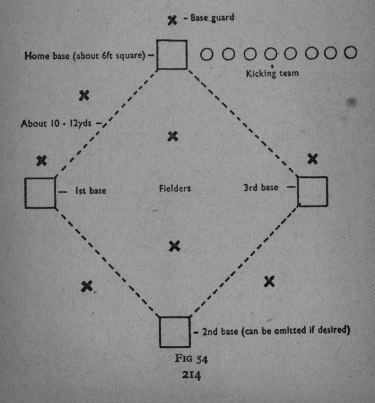

FIG 54
214

Two equal sides are formed, and a coin is tossed to determine the kicking and the fielding sides.

The Kicker places the ball in the Home Base, and then kicks it as far as he can forwards into the field of play.

If he can then run outside or through first, second, and third bases and back to the Home Base before the ball is returned to the Base Guard and placed or bounced by him in the base, one Home Run is scored.

If, however, the Kicker judges that he will not be able to make a Home Run, he can stop on any of the intermediate bases until such time as an opportunity to run occurs. Not more than two players may be at any one base at the same time.

If the Base Guard bounces the ball in the Home Base whilst any players are running between bases, those players are out.

A player who completes the circuit of the bases, but stops at one or more on the way round is allowed to kick again, but does not score a run.

Each side has the same number of innings (three or four), the one scoring the greatest number of Home Runs being the winner. Alternatively, three points can be given for a Home Run and one point for a safely completed circuit.

The length between bases can be varied to suit the ages of the players, and if so desired, the second base can be left out. With younger children this may well be advisable.

Circular Rounders (8 and to any age)

A simple form of rounders requiring either a small ball or an inflated beach ball. The court is marked out as shown in Fig 55.

Two equal teams are formed, and a coin is tossed to decide the fielding and striking sides. Each striking side then endeavours to score runs, the one making the greater number being the winner.

The fielding side 'Pitcher' throws the ball between waist and shoulder height to the Striker, who hits it with his hand as far as possible. He then tries to run all round the bases and back to behind the base line (course shown by dotted line) before the fielding side have passed the ball to Base One, Base Two, Base Three, and back to the Pitcher.

If, when the Striker hits the ball, it is caught by a fielder, the Striker is out.

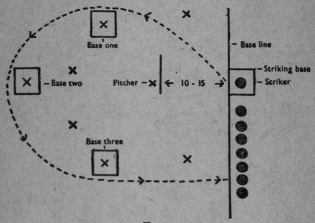

FIG 55

In this version of rounders no intermediate waiting at bases is allowed; once a ball has been struck by the Striker he must try to make a complete run.

The distances between bases will vary according to the age and capabilities of the players, but twenty-five to thirty feet is an average distance.

Arch-ball Rounders (8 to any age)

This game is a variation of *Circular Rounders*. The field of play is marked out in exactly the same way and the method of pitching, striking, and running is identical. The difference is in the method of fielding. Instead of the ball being thrown round the bases, it is returned immediately to the Pitcher. At the same time all the fielders rush to form a line behind him, and the ball is passed backwards, overhead down the line.

If it is received by the last man in the team before the Striker reaches the safety of the Base Line, he is out.

An alternative method of passing the ball down the line is underneath the legs. In such a case the game would then become *Tunnel-ball Rounders*.

Ring the Stick (8 to any age)

Two sticks and one rubber or rope quoit required. This team game, suitable for both boys and girls, is a variation of *Spade Ball* (*see* page 212).

A quoit is used instead of a ball, the object being to score points by throwing the quoit on to a stick held by a side's own goalkeeper, who is situated in the circle drawn in the opponent's half of the field.

The goalkeeper can assist by trying to catch the quoit on his own stick; he does not merely have to stand there holding the stick rigid.

All the other rules are as for *Spade Ball*.

Bucket Ball (8 and to any age)

Two small pails or buckets (the kind normally used on the beach) and a tennis ball or small rubber ball are required for this second variation of *Spade Ball*.

The object is to score goals by throwing the ball into a bucket held by your own goalkeeper, who is situated in the circle in your opponent's half of the field. As in *Ring the Stick*, the goalkeeper is allowed to take an active part in the game by trying to catch the ball in his bucket; he does not just have to stand passively holding the bucket, hoping that someone on his own side is an excellent shot. Again, all other rules are as for *Spade Ball*.

Hurly Burly (8 and to any age)

A team game for from five to eleven players a side. One ball of any size and a simple court marked as shown in Fig 56 are all that is required. The goals can be marked with pebbles, sticks, or spades.

Equal sides are picked and a coin is tossed for 'ends'. The object of the game is to score goals. The ball can be propelled by any method; it can be thrown, kicked, dribbled, run with as in Rugby, or headed. If a person who is carrying the ball is

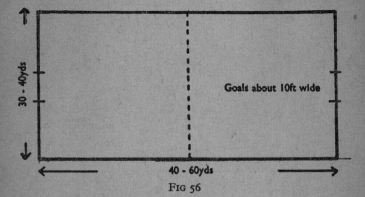

FIG 56

touched by a player from the opposing side he must pass the ball immediately. There must be no rough play; charging, pushing, shoving, and tackling are not allowed.

Play should continue for about ten minutes each way.

In scoring, the ball can be thrown or kicked through the goals or it can be carried through in the hands of a player.

Quoit Tennis (8 and to any age)

This game requires a quoit, a court, and a piece of string stretched between two canes at a height of about five feet. It is usually played by two or four players, but there is no reason why this should not be increased to six or eight, *ie* three or four a side.

The court is marked out to the approximate sizes shown in Fig 57. These can be varied at will to suit both the age and skill of the players.

218

Rules

(1) The scoring is as in Lawn Tennis.

(2) The service is made, as in tennis, from the base line, underarm. The arm must not be raised above shoulder height.

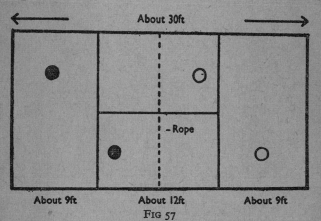

About 30ft

- Rope

About 9ft   About 12ft   About 9ft

Fig 57

(3) To be valid, the serve must be into the appropriate service court area.

(4) Two serves are allowed. 'Lets' as in Tennis.

(5) The quoit must be caught one handed.

(6) Once the quoit is caught, no movement of the feet is allowed, and the quoit must be returned immediately.

(7) A point is lost if the quoit touches the floor, is returned under the 'net', or if it is thrown out of court.

Pebble Golf

A pleasant 'after the meal' or 'before the swim' game which doesn't involve father in too much energy is *Pebble Golf*. A number of holes, say nine, about six inches across and six inches deep are dug on the beach at varying distances apart from thirty to one hundred yards. Small sandcastle flags are placed in the sand close to the holes to indicate their positions.

Players then select round pebbles about the size of a cricket ball. (Older or stronger players can have heavier ones than the younger children.) These pebbles are then rolled or thrown underarm, the object being, as in golf, to go round the course in as few strokes (or throws) as possible.

With younger children (under ten) the distances between the 'holes' can be shortened and a circle of about three feet diameter used instead of a small sunken hole.

Camp Golf

This is a variation of *Pebble Golf* for use at Scout or Guide camps. Groundsheets are used as 'holes', and enamel or tin plates skimmed through the air instead of pebbles. When plates are used the 'course' immediately ahead must be clear of other players, and the 'missiles' must be kept at below waist height.

Picnic Occupations

Most of the outdoor games mentioned in this book can be played on picnics both on the beach and in the country. In between these more strenuous activities, to give you a rest and the children a change, it is often a good thing to organise simple competitions in which the children go off and work on their own or with a partner.

A small prize, be it only a bar of chocolate or an extra bottle of lemonade, makes an additional incentive far beyond the actual value of the reward. Here are some suggestions for the beach and the country. A time and space limit should be set, otherwise you are liable to spend the rest of the day looking for wandering children.

BEACH COMPETITIONS

(1) Collect as many different kinds of seaweed as you can in half an hour.

(2) Collect as many different kinds of shells as you can.

(3) Collect as many different kinds of pebbles as you can.

(4) See who can find a pebble that looks most like a golf ball or a tennis ball.

(5) See who can collect three pebbles that look most like birds' eggs.

(6) See who can collect the most curious looking pebble.

(7) See who can find the largest piece of wood.

(8) See who can collect the largest number of corks.

(9) See who can collect the largest number of limpet shells (or the biggest limpet shell).

(10) See which pair can make the biggest castle in half an hour.

(11) Build a sandcastle that looks like a real castle.

(12) Build a circular sand wall at the edge of the sea (when the tide is coming in) and see whose wall lasts the longest.

(13) Work in pairs or threes. Build a castle near the water's edge and stick a small flag on top of it. The one whose flag is the last to be knocked down by the sea is the winner. (This is sometimes known as 'Tide Fight'.)

(14) See who can build the best motor boat or motor car out of sand.

(15) See who can make the longest line of pebbles in fifteen minutes. Each pebble must touch the next.

(16) See who can make the largest number of sand pies in ten minutes.

(17) See who can dig the deepest hole in a quarter of an hour. (Work in pairs or threes.)

(18) See who can collect the largest number of crabs, shrimps, small fish, etc, in thirty minutes. This can be varied according to location, eg the biggest crab, the largest shrimp, the most starfish, etc.

(19) Collect as many feathers as you can in twenty minutes.

(20) Collect as many different kinds of flowers or grasses (where there are sandhills) as you can in half an hour.

COUNTRYSIDE OCCUPATIONS

(1) Collect as many different kinds of flowers as you can.

(2) See who can find the biggest leaf.

(3) Collect as many different kinds of leaves (or grasses) as you can in half an hour.

(4) Collect as many different blue (pink, red, yellow) flowers as you can.

(5) See how many birds' nests you can find. (Don't touch them.)

(6) Collect the biggest bunch of buttercups or daisies.

(7) Gather as many different kinds of berries as you can. (Warn them not to try to eat any of them—particularly Deadly Nightshade.)

(8) For young girls. See who can make the longest daisy chain in twenty minutes.

(9) See who can make the longest and neatest plait from rushes.

(10) Stalking and tracking games and competitions can also be organised, *eg* the 'scout' sits in the centre of an open space. The remainder disappear out of sight and then try to get as near to him as possible without being seen. Anyone who is spotted joins the 'scout' and helps him to spot the others. At the end of a specified time (quarter to half an hour) the 'scout' shouts 'Time up' or blows a whistle. All those remaining unseen then stand up, or disclose themselves; the one who is nearest to the 'scout' is the winner and becomes the 'scout' for the next turn. Some of the more enthusiastic ones will try to camouflage themselves with grasses and leaves. This can be suggested at the beginning of the game.

THESE ARE 🔲 PAN BOOKS

Hubert Phillips

THE PAN QUIZ BOOK

A Pan Original. Fifty sets of twenty questions and
answers, covering history, literature, astronomy, biol-
ogy, geography and other subjects. By a famous 'Round
Britain Quiz' expert. (2/6)

Hubert Phillips

THE PAN BOOK OF CARD GAMES

Britain's leading authority tells you how to play all the
popular card games—and introduces many new ones.
With its innumerable specimen hands, played out card
by card, and its lucid explanations—this famous book is
both entertaining and instructive. (3/6)

John S. Vinden, FZS

THE PAN BOOK OF THE HOME
AQUARIUM

A Pan Original. A new ABC of fishkeeping specially
written for PAN by a Fellow of the Zoological Society.
For the beginner and for the enthusiast—a comprehen-
sive guide to one of today's simplest, most fascinating
hobbies. (2/6)

Sacheverell Sitwell

BRITISH ARCHITECTS AND CRAFTSMEN

For every lover of beauty and tradition. The best
written and illustrated book on the subject—a classic.
'A 'must' book'—*Sunday Graphic. Illustrated.* (5/-)

PICK OF THE PAPERBACKS

THESE ARE ◼ PAN BOOKS